Round the Circle: Doulas Share Their Experiences

Julie Brill, CCCE, CLD

Round the Circle: Doulas Share Their Experiences

Julie Brill, CCCE, CLD

© Copyright 2015

WellPregnancy Press

Library of Congress Control Number: 2014956169

ISBN-13: 978-1-9398474-4-7

Dedication

To doulas everywhere who choose this path that requires working unknown hours at unscheduled times, and who pursue continuing education to continually offer better service out of a desire to truly support women during the childbearing year, thank you.

To women who feel called to support other women and their families during this time of transition, surrender, and growth, even if you do not yet call yourself a doula. The most important act we do as doulas is show up with our hearts and hands. Start where you are, you are enough.

To the mothers who share this personal time and their innermost thoughts and fears with us, you are our greatest teachers.

Acknowledgements

Thank you to:

My parents, Haim and Martha Brill, who taught me to believe that any achievement is possible. My mother is also the designer of the *Round the Circle* cover.

My daughters, Rebecca and Sophie, who were so excited about and interested in this project.

My brother, Alex Brill, who helped me with the contract end of creating this anthology.

Micky Jones, whom I bumped into again and again at the 2013 CAPPA Conference, for inspiring me with her own book project and supporting me while I took this leap.

Paula Jordan, Laurel Wilson, Tracy Wilson Peters, and Jennifer Sahn, who encouraged me.

Janet Rourke, my editor, who patiently answered my questions.

All of the contributors who gave their time and expertise so generously and made this project - a gift to the doula community - possible. I am honored by all that you shared and to be a part of your community.

And I am forever grateful to my mentors, student childbirth educator and labor doulas, and the pregnant families I have worked with - you are all my greatest teachers.

What I Wish I Had Known When I Was a New Doula

"I wish I had known how to manage when I joined a client better. At first I would take off to join them at pretty much the first sign of labor. After being with my first three clients for an average of 30 hours each.... I decided to be more judicious about the timing of it all."

Jessica Fuss, Soft Touch Doula Services, Certified Birth Doula

"I wish I knew that I didn't have to make birth perfect in MY eyes for everyone. That even when a woman has a cesarean, it can be a positive birth memory. And that I met Polly Perez sooner, who taught me about responsible TO or responsible FOR."

Crystal R. Sada, CLD, CCCE

"That normal birth can take minutes or days. That dilation is irrelevant to progression. That mothers are commonly deceived into thinking their body isn't working or their baby isn't thriving at end of pregnancy and in labor. That VBAC moms are just moms and work the same as every other mom. That staying home until late in labor is critical for any mother having a longer labor and desiring to avoid cesarean and birth normally. That the words used around pregnant and birthing mothers are critical to their perception of a happy experience."

Khadijah Cisse, Birth Guide

"Being a doula is not a job, it is a lifestyle. It will take priority over everything, including friends, family, and personal time, but it is also so rewarding. When your clients experience trauma during difficult births, it stays with you. Processing what you experienced is key."

Charity Parrott, Doula, CBE, Licensed Massage Therapist

"I wish I had known how to set better boundaries, and that it's perfectly acceptable to ask clients to call during normal business hours unless they are in labor or have another urgent matter."

Christa Bartley, RN, Doula

"I wish I'd taken more time to research my certifying agency. There is a difference in quality. It's not just about the letters behind your name, it's about how you can use that information to make you successful - not only as support for your clients, but also as a business person."

Jenn Leonard, Homebirth Doula and CBE

"I wish I had known that good marketing skills are vital to your success."

Amy Peterson, CD (DONA), CLC Hound Hill Doula

"I wish I had known that watching, listening, and feeling for ten minutes before DOING can be one's most valuable tool while showing up with heart-centered presence."

Sandra Florez-Lujan, DONA Trained Birth Doula

"I wish I had not been afraid that I would not have been Enough.

As a new doula, I had training to support with information - with experience I gained the wisdom to open my mind to many individual options and to hold the choices made and the results lightly.

As a new doula, I was eager to support emotionally - with experience I added the wisdom to know when just to be there and when touch was needed.

As a new doula, I had the strong hands and back to support physically - I learned my muscle best exercised was a strong, warm and peaceful heart.

Do not be afraid - just show up with all you have and with all you can grow into being, and you will be Enough."

Terri Woods, CLD, CD (DONA), CAPPA Labor Doula Faculty

Table of Contents

Introduction

Julie Brill, CCCE, CLD

Fixing It Before It's Broken

You are holding in your hands a doula mentorship in a book. If you're a new or newer doula, you're part of the second generation of professional support for women and their partners. Hopefully, you're benefiting from the hard work of the doulas who have come before you, who worked to establish this field. As doulas have become more well known in my area, I no longer spend so much time explaining what a doula does or even spelling the word for people. As more families choose to labor and birth with doulas, there is more work for an increasing number of doulas. The benefits for families are innumerable. As doulas we have the opportunity to be there at the beginning, to literally fix it before it's broken, one mother, one baby, one family at a time. My vision is to share what experienced doulas learned the hard way and to facilitate providing the birth community with a book full of sisterly support.

Round the Circle takes its name from my image of a group of doulas sitting in a circle, sharing their wisdom. There's the feeling to me of informality and of woman-to-woman learning in a non-hierarchical setting. At my doula and childbirth trainings, and in my childbirth classes, we sit in a circle, never in rows, because a circle facilitates the flow of information. I believe that learning occurs in a circular or spiral fashion, not in a linear way. By that I mean we typically learn something about a topic, then come back to it later, and that knowledge gets reinforced and deepened. Then we go on, coming by that topic again and again. Additionally, the circle is a very female shape, and pregnancy is a time of rounding. Also, rounding the circle can be like rounding the bend, where we come forward and encounter something we didn't know was there, or we go on to a different part of our journey. But rounding the circle can also be perfecting the shape of something. A circle should be round, and the more we learn, the more we perfect the craft of doulaing. The rounder our knowledge, the more we have to offer. I hope this anthology will help you round out your doula skills.

This book came together like a potluck, where everyone brings their best dish. Somehow the desserts are balanced out by soups and salads, and the whole meal harmonizes with no organization from the hostess. I am honored and lucky to have worked with so many amazing doulas, who generously shared their time, wrote about their experiences, and worked to meet my deadlines. What a treat to come to my inbox time and again to discover more inspiring ideas and heartfelt stories. Thanks so much to all of you.

I am so honored by the doulas who submitted such beautiful work for this collaboration. Some doulas I know because I trained them, others are my fellow CAPPA Faculty members. Sometimes I approached a doula whose work I admired and asked her to submit, and she did! Others heard about the project through Facebook, or through word of mouth, that ever-present current in the birth community.

As I worked to select chapters, I thought about what I wish I had known when I attended my first birth in 1992, and what questions new doulas frequently ask me at trainings and as they begin to attend births. But the reality is that as doulas we never complete our education, and so I also considered the questions we all think about and live with. The most important thing we do as doulas is to show up, physically and mentally, bringing our minds, our hearts, and our hands ready to help in any way we can, ready to provide non-judgmental support. No matter how much you have learned, and how much you have yet to discover, that is enough.

Fear in birth and how to help is a perennial topic in the birth community. Nancy Abbott begins this anthology by pointing out the elephant in the room, and helping us to address it and help our moms move past it. She shares how to go beyond comfort measures and help our clients get their jobs done.

Laurel Wilson and Tracy Wilson Peters explain the latest research on the mother-baby bond and how what we think during pregnancy literally shapes our babies. They describe how doulas can help clients with this process, especially when they are able to connect with them early in pregnancy.

Amy Wright Glenn and Kristen Avonti address how to support a woman's spirit before, during, and after labor - an important but often neglected aspect of doulaing.

Teresa Howard, Tara Campbell, Robin Gray-Reed, and Kim Bradlee address how to help women in specific circumstances, such as pushing before the provider is present, a cesarean birth, or a homebirth.

Jenny King and Amy L. Gilliland write about working with friends. Ann E. Tohill provides recipes and tips for helping the postpartum family.

Amy Mager, Rachel Hess, Kay Miller, Vickie Elson, Renà Koerner, and Darla Burns share how to work with specific populations, including observant Jewish families, LGBTQ families, teen moms, immigrants, women who are incarcerated, and families involved with surrogacy.

Ready to take your doula work to the next level? Rivka Cymbalist contributes what she has learned about creating and maintaining a volunteer program. Kimberly Bepler shares what she knows about growing a business and I share about marketing. Lois Brown Loar discusses what she discovered about running her doula business from watching her dad manage his hardware store. Charlotte Scott writes about doulaing yourself.

Jeannette LeBlanc said, "A circle of women may just be the most powerful force known to humanity. If you have one, embrace it. If you need one, seek it. If you find one, for the love of all that is good and holy, dive in. Hold on. Love it up. Get naked. Let them see you. Let them hold you. Let your reluctant tears fall. Let yourself rise fierce and love gentle. You will be changed. The very fabric of your being will be altered by this if you allow it. Please, please allow it."

Thank you for being part of this circle.

Chapter 1

The Role of the Doula: What's Fear Got to Do With It?

Nancy Abbott, CD (DONA)

Several years ago, my family and I were in a terrible car accident. What does this have to do with being a doula? Give me a minute and I'll tell you.

My husband, daughter, and I were driving from Illinois to New Hampshire. It was 2:30 a.m. and I fell asleep at the wheel. We didn't hit anyone, thank the Lord, but our vehicle flipped all the way over, and our daughter was expelled into the median strip. My husband and I were not seriously hurt, but our daughter went through extensive surgeries. She was in a wheelchair for three months. It was a devastating and traumatic experience.

Every time I looked at my daughter in that wheelchair, every time I saw her in pain, I said to myself, "I feel so ashamed. What kind of mother am I? I did that to her!" A friend of mine heard me say this, and she said, "It was an accident. Don't feel that way!"

Don't feel that way? Okay. Where is the control knob that I can turn the emotion off? I would be glad not to feel that way. But I did.

Because I am a doula, I began to relate this experience to what I do in the labor room, as I do with most things in life. When I am with a laboring mother, and I see fear on her face, I am tempted to say, "Don't be afraid!" And she could very well say back to me, "Okay, where is the control knob?" "Don't be afraid" is one of the most ridiculous things you can say to anyone who is dealing with fear. And yet when fear raises its head in the labor room, we are tempted to say it. When I walk into a laboring mom's room, and I see fear on her face, what should I do? I can't just make it go away with a simple reassurance. So, after my car accident, I began to formulate a way to deal with fear during childbirth.

Purpose of a Doula

First of all, before I did anything else, I had to reaffirm my purpose in the room. Why was I there in the first place? I am not there to see to it that the mom has a "natural childbirth." I am not there to see to it that she has a healthy baby. I am not there to insure that the hospital personnel can do their jobs efficiently. There may be elements of all of these in what I actually do there, but what is my primary purpose in the labor room?

A doula is there to provide a "presence" in a woman's labor, and whether she's laboring in a living room, the sidewalk outside, or the triage cubicle of the local hospital, a doula is there to BE. She provides the one focused and consistent presence in the room, with her focus on the laboring mom, and no other. Plenty of other people are there to do specific jobs. Doctors, midwives, and nurses come and go. The doula stays. She doesn't have "call time." She doesn't say, "Well, I have been here for 24 hours. It's time for me to go." This is one of the hallmarks of doula care: consistent support and focus. The doula isn't distracted by others, by her own private life, by any other stimulation in the room or the environment. She should have all of her attention squarely on the laboring mother, anticipating needs, and then meeting them, to the best of her ability. She must be totally "present." She is there to BE.

With this consistent presence in the room, the laboring mother can then feel free to concentrate on the job at hand. She knows that all is right with her world. She is there to accomplish a job, and the doula's presence encourages her to feel prepared to do that job.

My own midwife liked to knit. When the labor didn't need her active hand, she sat in the corner and knitted quietly. I could hear the soft "click-click-click" of her knitting needles. Her quiet presence was so empowering. It freed me up to labor without fear.

A doula is a tool to be used toward birth satisfaction. By this I don't mean that having a doula means everything is going to go beautifully. I wish it did. Birth satisfaction means the mom is satisfied that every choice she made is the best one she could have made at the time. The birth that she experienced may not be what she wished for or anticipated, but as she faced each choice, each decision, she is confident, satisfied that she made good choices and that she was an active participant in her childbirth experience.

When I met with Shelley prenatally, she told me she had formulated her birth plan. She was going to get to 5 cm, and then ask for the epidural. That was her plan. After making sure that she understood this choice, describing an epidural labor to her, she seemed confident that this was the labor she wanted. When she called me to her labor, I went to her home, and we labored there for several hours. When we finally got to the hospital, she was examined and told that she was 9½ cm dilated. She sat up in the labor bed and said, "Okay. I want my epidural now." The doctor and nurse both pooh-poohed this, waving away her request. They thought she was doing fine, so why change anything? But I was looking at her face, and she was visibly shaken. Someone had just taken her birth plan and thrown it out the window, and the words "birth satisfaction" were going through my head. So I sat down next to her, took her hands in mine, and said, "You can have the epidural, Shelley, but I want you to know something: it will probably take effect after the baby's here." She contemplated this for a minute, and then said, "Well, okay. What should I do now?" I suggested we walk the halls for a couple of minutes, and then come back to the room and have the baby. And that is exactly what we did. So, what did I do? I made sure the choice remained in her hands. That is the surest way toward birth satisfaction.

A doula offers physical, mental, informational, and emotional support to women in labor. That takes a lot of presence: physical - a hug, a massage, a cool cloth; mental - seeing what the mom is doing, anticipating what she may need next; informational - discussing options, offering opinions when asked; emotional - simply loving her.

A good doula does not "check out." She doesn't go off to the cafeteria for an hour. She doesn't wrap herself in a sheet and take a nap. She needs to eat and rest, yes - but not at the expense of her focus. She should be actively present from the first time the mom asks for her, until mom and baby are happily bonding, ready for rest and quiet.

I recently had a birth where the laboring mom and her partner kept asking me to step outside the room. I was in the hall more than I was in the labor room. Three times I was asked, by three different doctors, "What are you doing out here?" When I explained that the couple wanted some space, all three doctors had the same reaction. "Doesn't this couple understand what you DO?" I was there in whatever capacity the couple wanted, but no, I don't think they really understood my function.

A doula is a tool. The laboring woman brings tools to her labor. The classes she takes, the partner she brings, the books she reads, and her doula are all tools to use as she works through her labor. As I work prenatally with a mother, I ask her reason for requesting a doula. Nine times out of ten, the mom says "support." She understands there are no guarantees in this process. I can't promise that everything will go swimmingly. Wouldn't that be nice? But I can promise that whatever she goes through, I go through it with her - every move, every breath, every touch.

The very first time I attended a birth as a doula was in 1971. I had never heard the word "doula" back then. I was a newly trained Lamaze "labor coach." The laboring mom was a fourteen-year-old girl. She was scared and alone. Relatively speaking, I knew nothing. Oh, I could "hut-hut-hoo" with the best of them, but I had no experience at all. Not once had I ever been in a labor room. I hadn't even had a baby of my own yet. (I have since had six!)

So what did I have to offer this sweet, young girl? Gentle, encouraging words; a warm soft touch. I was there to wrap my arms around her and ride the waves of labor with her. In other words, I was offering her my presence.

Once I was sure of my purpose in the process, I could then address dealing with fear. As a doula in the labor room, I may find I need to sort out what is going on in a mom's mind. I often ask, "What was going through your mind during that last contraction?" The responses are many and varied, but I think I can boil them down to several specific types of fear or anxiety.

Fear of the Length of Labor

Most often, the mom is worried she will not be able to have the endurance to labor peacefully. The labor can often challenge her, and she thinks it will challenge her beyond her ability to deal with it. "I don't know how much more of this I can do," she says. Right then and there, I see that her mind has gone beyond the moment. I want her in the present, not worried about three hours from now. So I need to bring her back to the "here and now." I begin with changing her position. If she is lying down, I get her up. If she is standing up, I sit her down. I move her to a different place in the room; I put her into a different physical position. Then I tell her what we will be doing for the next ten minutes. We will address each contraction with a new breathing pattern, a new massage, a new visualization. What have I just done? I have changed her focus. I can't change her challenging labor, but I have just given her four different ways to deal with it. I have also given her a short-term goal. Now she is not thinking about three hours from now. She has been brought back to the present. I continue to do this throughout the labor, and with the options I present to her, her self-confidence builds. "I did the last one; I can do the next one. Beyond that I need not worry."

Fear of Interventions

I also find moms who are worried about what the medical personnel will suggest. "I want to labor unmolested," said one mom. She may be right to be concerned. What a doula needs to do in this case is to remind the mom that she always has a voice. If there is something amiss with her or the baby, then her options are limited, but that is when a doula can help. Not necessarily to provide answers to questions, as much as to help her know what questions to ask, and what her options might be.

Lisa called me one day:

"They are going to induce me on Monday," she said.

"Oh, really? Why?" I asked.

"Because I have high blood pressure."

"Do you arrive at your appointments straight from work at lunch time?" I asked her.

"Yes," she responded.

"Maybe you should try getting there at another time of day," I suggest. "Now, why Monday?"

"Because my doctor is at the hospital on Monday."

"Oh, really? So, you're having this medical intervention simply because the doctor is there that day?"

"Um, yes."

"Okay. Now there are at least four different medical methods of induction. Which one are they suggesting you use?"

"I…don't know. No one told me any of that."

"Oh, really? Well, let me tell you what is available to you, as well as the non-medical methods. Then maybe you can discuss with your doctor the pros and cons of each one."

In this situation I am arming her with information and options. That is a huge part of a doula's job. The more options she is presented with, the more comfortable she will be with the decisions she helps to make.

Fear of the Challenge of Labor

A good time to address some of the thoughts that could potentially run through a mother's mind when she goes into labor is before the labor actually begins. I often start in my prenatal visit by going over what a contraction might feel like. I have had women describe a contraction; here are some of their descriptions:

Really strong menstrual cramps.

Pressure from the inside moving outward, such as a balloon inflating and deflating.

Pressure from the outside moving inward, such as a boa constrictor squeezing and relaxing.

The baby itself moving outward and downward, as though the baby were putting its feet on her ribcage and stretching.

A bowling ball dropping into a corset.

The planet Saturn. (I love this one!) Imagine pressure that starts way down low, and then moves upward, wrapping around the mom's body in giant circles.

In my prenatal sessions, after talking about these sensations, I remind the mom of what brings dilation: good, strong, rhythmical contractions. We want them close together, consistent, and productive. During really strong labor, these feelings intensify. So when they come closer and closer, stronger and stronger, we greet them with enthusiasm. If a mom isn't prepared to have such sensations, she can begin to feel quite overwhelmed. It would be counterproductive to bring those particular sensations up at this point during labor, but I simply say, "Do you remember the talk we had a month ago about what a contraction feels like? Isn't it wonderful that your body knows what to do? Welcome each one."

Susan had gotten to the pushing stage of her labor. She was moving the baby down the birth canal quite nicely. She was sitting on the side of the bed, with her husband behind her, supporting her back. I was sitting on the floor, right in front of her. My head was level with her perineum, so I had a perfect view of the top of the baby's head as it moved closer and closer. At first I could see just about a dime's size of the baby's head, but little by little I could see more and more. Susan was doing a perfect job, but at one point, as she pushed long and steadily, the baby's head disappeared backup the vaginal canal…while she pushed. That's strange, I thought. I'm supposed to be seeing more and more, but instead I'm seeing less and less. I asked her what was going through her mind as she pushed. She said to me, "I feel so much pressure; I think I'm going to split in two!" This is a very common fear. It would be counterproductive to plant that thought into her mind, but once it is there, it must be dealt with. I suggested Susan do several things: with her next push, I suggested she visualize getting into an elevator and going down to the basement; while she pushed, I asked her to drop her chin down slowly, then I asked that she spread her elbows out, ready to open her arms for her baby. I told her the pressure she was feeling was the door her baby had to go through. "Open that door," I said. I didn't tell her not to be afraid. I gave her three things to do to handle those sensations and she delivered beautifully ten minutes later.

I want a mom to understand that the sensations of labor are not something she should try to avoid or diminish. I got a call one day from a woman who was looking for a doula. She told me she was going to talk to ten doulas on the phone, and then from those ten, she would pick three she wanted to meet face-to-face. Would I be willing to spend some time on the phone with her? I said sure. We talked together for forty-five minutes. At the end of our conversation, she said I was one of the doulas she wanted to meet face-to-face because I sounded different from any other doula she had talked to. I sheepishly asked, "In what way?" She said, "Because all of the other doulas I've spoken with, all they talked about were comfort measures. You're the only doula who has said to me, 'You've got a job to do. Let's get it done!'"

Acknowledging what labor actually is goes a long way to reassuring the mom that what she is going through is normal and necessary. It's easier to deal with if she understands exactly what her body is doing. I often use the illustration of the baby in a crocheted pillowcase, with a turtleneck. If we want to get the baby out of the pillowcase, not only does the turtleneck have to open, but the baby has to be urged downward, as well. That is labor: open and urge. Open and urge. Open and urge. I encourage the mom to accept it. Be ready for it. Welcome it.

Fear for Baby's Wellbeing

Another common source of anxiety for some pregnant women is worrying about the health and wellbeing of her unborn child. Until she can actually hold her little one in her arms, counting all the fingers and toes, she worries - especially during labor. Some women love to be monitored. They're reassured by hearing the lub-dub of the fetal heart rate. I also often ask the nurse or doctor to periodically say the baby seems to be doing beautifully. "Is my baby all right?" a mom might ask. I smile and say, "If anyone thought the baby was in trouble, this room would be full of people. The fact that we are here quietly laboring is a sign that all is well."

Prenatally, I start by discussing nutrition, exercise, rest, and fluid intake. More than likely, their own doctor or midwife has discussed this with them - at least they should have. However, a mom may need more reaffirmation she is doing everything she can to provide the baby with a good start. I sometimes mention my own children. Five of my six kids had significant health issues of one kind or another, and yet there was not a thing I could have done prenatally to prevent any of it - nothing. I make sure the mom is given a list of things she can do to the best of her ability to give her baby the best start. Then, if the baby is born with issues, you cry, you say a prayer, and then you get up and take care of the baby knowing you have done all you could.

Nothing to Fear but Fear Itself

Simply put, fear is the absence of peace. I am a woman of great faith and my faith is my source for peace. A doula should be able to sit peacefully with a laboring mom. She should bring her own peace into the room. If she has no confidence in the laboring process, she is in the wrong line of work. The woman's body was created to do this. It wants to accomplish the task of childbirth. Yes, things sometimes go amiss, but that is also the time when the mom needs a peaceful presence in the room - someone who can put her arms around her, sharing her strength. This, above all, dispels fear.

I urge a mother to find her center: her source for peace, and then transmit that to her unborn child. There is no greater gift you can give your child, besides the gift of life, than to share with your little one your own inner strength and peace. What a great way to begin motherhood. I am very humbled by the fact that I get to witness this every time I attend a birth. I have the best job in the world!

· · · · · ·

While Nancy Abbott, CD (DONA), was pregnant with her first child in 1971, she trained and certified as a Lamaze labor coach. She has since been recertified by DONA. Now as a mother of six, and a grandmother of six (so far), she continues to

Nancy Abbott and Toyin Ikwuakor

Photo by AK Ikwuakor.
Used with permission.

offer emotional, physical, and informational support to women in labor. She is familiar with HypnoBirthing, Mindful Childbirth, Birthing From Within, the Bradley method, and Lamaze. She uses a combination of all of these while she watches miracles happen. After attending hundreds of births, she continues to have a profound respect for the strength of a woman's body and the soundness of her spirit. Nancy lives in Derry, New Hampshire, with her husband and youngest daughter.

Chapter 2

The Doula's Role in Influencing the Mother-Baby Bond

Laurel Wilson, IBCLC, CLE, CCCE, CLD

Tracy Wilson Peters, CLE, CCCE, CLD

When Does Mothering Really Begin?

Most people believe mothering begins when a baby is born, but many doulas will tell you a different story - that mothering begins early in pregnancy. Beginning at conception, women need to be mothered while we mother our babies. Doula relationships ideally start early in pregnancy, so the doula is available as a mentor, support person, and gentle guide through this transition.

Some women feel mothering began when they first learned they were pregnant. Others say it began when they felt their baby move for the first time, heard the heartbeat, or saw their baby on ultrasound. There are those who felt the stirring of mothering begin when they held their babies for the first time. There are also women who did not feel truly like mothers until their babies were days or even weeks old.

"I have a very difficult time wrapping my mind around the very idea of pregnancy - even as I feel my little one moving around. I can't say that I really felt bonded with my babies until the moment of birth - and then it was immediate and incredible." – Emily

While it is normal to begin to "feel" like a mother at different stages, new evidence shows that mothering in a biological sense begins at the moment of conception. The mother-baby bond occurs before a mother may feel an emotional connection to her baby (Wilson & Wilson Peters, 2012, 2014). In her book, *The Tentative Pregnancy*, Barbara Katz Rothman discovered some women prevent themselves from connecting to their babies until after all of the early pregnancy tests and/or screenings have gone well and they enter into the second trimester. They often believe some magic occurs at 12 to 16 weeks, so it becomes safe to announce their pregnancies. Whether the mother's emotional connection starts early in pregnancy or much later, there is a mind/body/spirit bond beginning between her and her baby from the earliest point of pregnancy.

Most doula relationships start early in the third trimester. This poses a dilemma for doulas who really want to help shape a positive mother-baby bond for their clients throughout pregnancy. How can doulas share the message of the importance of early connection and awareness when they are not even beginning a relationship until late in pregnancy? Doula support could be critical in the first trimester when women are often so fearful about what may lie ahead. Is it time to expand the role of the doula? Should doula care begin earlier in pregnancy? Should there be early pregnancy doulas?

A global understanding of what the mother-baby bond means for the health and happiness of children could change how society begins to think about the role of mothering. What the world needs is a pregnancy paradigm shift. The doula world also needs to experience this shift. Cutting-edge research has discovered that the experience in the womb, the early moments of birth, and early infancy are the most formative moments in our lives (Hobel & Culhane, 2003: Marsh, Gerber & Peterson, 2008; O'Rahilly & Mueller, 2008; Simmons, 2011). These quantum moments shape all that we become. Everything from what a mother eats and drinks, to the relationships she has during pregnancy, to her stress levels are influencing her developing baby. If the definition of mothering is the nurturing of a child, a pregnant woman is literally mothering from the time of conception. If the doula's role is to mother the mother, then this relationship also needs to begin early in pregnancy.

It's now exceedingly difficult for mothers to have the opportunity to truly connect with their babies during pregnancy. Today's millennial families are experiencing more stimulus than ever. They are constantly connected to data, information, texts, email, phone calls, and messaging literally everywhere. The pace of life has sped up significantly, and what is expected of a pregnant mother today - the literal demands on her time and energy - has increased exponentially. It is easy for pregnant women to begin to live on autopilot, becoming more susceptible to media and other external messages, and less able to connect with their own thoughts and feelings. Pregnant mothers who take the time to become aware of their thoughts, feelings, and actions begin to become more conscious of their behaviors. When women take advantage of forging relationships with their doulas early on, they can have expert guidance during this impactful period.

In our technology-obsessed world, it is easy for mothers to forget the most important knowledge comes from within. In our society it is rare that women listen to their bodies' cues and respond to them. How many pregnant mothers nap during the day when they are tired? They avoid listening to their bodies because they feel rushed and don't honor their bodies' signals as actual communications. The pregnant body is communicating what it needs all the time, and believe it or not, the unborn baby is too. All mothers have to do is learn to listen. They must give themselves permission to trust the mother-baby connection and take the time to respond. This is something that doulas can remind mothers to do - listen to their bodies and intuition.

Doulas are also becoming more and more technologically dependent with their clients. More doulas are communicating via text, instead of making real connections with the women they serve. We seem to be leaving behind the days of meeting over tea and scones and really forging a bond between the doula and the mother. Have doulas underestimated their own importance? The relationships we have with our clients are not only important, they are influential. When we use technological shortcuts, we miss out on the development of these relationships. When there is actual in-person contact, a deeper relationship is occurring. Communication at this level involves not only voice, but also eye contact and often touch, and results in oxytocin release in both the mother and the doula, which deepens the mother/doula bond and influences the mother-baby bond. Mothers who feel more supported and cared for are more able to focus inward and bond more effectively with their babies.

Why Does Mothering Begin at Conception?

Nature is impressive in its design. From the moment of conception, it prepares babies to survive and thrive in the new world they will encounter beginning at birth. The information babies receive from their mothers in utero teaches them how to adapt. The mother is constantly communicating all that she knows about her world to her baby throughout pregnancy, via special messenger molecules. This is one of her early mothering abilities - to share her feelings with her baby. The baby communicates back to the mother through the placenta, with his own set of messenger molecules. Mom and baby share information and love during each and every moment of pregnancy. This mother-baby bond is the foundation of what we call attachment pregnancy.

This biological communication between a mother and her baby is how the baby's emotional intelligence is created. He experiences the world of emotions through his mother. He begins to become aware of his mother's world based on how she feels about her world. When she has a loving thought, he experiences love. When she is stressed, he becomes stressed. Babies have the opportunity to experience an array of emotions and develop a healthy emotional life that matches the emotional tone of his new family. This emotional tone is his way of coping with his world, known as the EQ or emotional quotient. New research has shown a healthy EQ is much more important for long-term happiness than a high IQ.

If mothers were aware of the early influence they have on their babies' personality and health, they would likely spend more time doing things they enjoy instead of focusing on less important tasks, like worrying over what color to paint the nursery. Doulas have a unique opportunity to educate families on this information. When we begin supporting clients early in pregnancy, we share this important information about mindful mothering.

Mindful Prenatal Mothering

Awareness of the mother-baby bond is crucial for creating a more peaceful society. Pregnancy is when conscious mothering begins. When babies are conceived and develop in a trusting, peaceful, loving state, they are literally formed in love. Early pregnancy is an ideal time for mothers to contemplate their relationship with themselves and the world around them. This involves moving into a state of observation and awareness, and becoming mindful. Jon Kabat-Zinn, author of *Everyday Blessings* and known as the modern day guru of mindfulness, defines mindfulness as the following, "Mindfulness means paying attention in a particular way; on purpose, in the present moment, and nonjudgmentally."

What mothers think about, they bring about. Therefore, it makes sense for doulas to help mothers learn how to become more mindful. A mother's experience impacts the health and personality of her baby. Mothers can make decisions that are truly in their best interest by being in conscious agreement. What is conscious agreement? It is the act of making decisions based on deep, inner listening, and coming to an intuitive mind/body/spirit agreement. It is making decisions that feel good at a gut level. Conscious agreement occurs when you are in collaboration with your inner wisdom, when every part of you says "YES!" The word agreement literally means being in harmony with one's feelings. If there was just one concept that all doulas should be teaching their clients, it is that of conscious agreement.

Before pregnancy, a woman's consciousness mainly affects her own life. Once she conceives, she must acknowledge that her consciousness impacts her baby's development and emotional health. All her choices, from what she eats, to what she does, to the people she allows in her life (co-workers, healthcare providers, friends, and partners) impact her baby. Every moment in her life affects her emotional state. Being in a state of conscious agreement during pregnancy (and even while trying to conceive) becomes vital to the mother-baby connection.

Teaching conscious agreement is easy. Teach mothers to follow four steps:

1. Separate from external influences: To make a decision based on conscious agreement, it is sometimes necessary to remove yourself from environments or people that may be distracting. This can be as simple as closing your eyes and taking a moment to connect to your inner wisdom.

2. Get quiet and pause: Take a few deep breaths; allow your thoughts to calm and connect to your source. Your source can be defined as that which guides you - God, the universe, your spirit, your intuition, etc.

3. Listen in: Think about the situation that has presented itself. What is your gut feeling? How is your body feeling? How is your body reacting? Do you feel drawn to the situation or person, or do you feel a sense of discomfort? How might your baby feel?

4. Decide and commit: Honor the feelings that are coming up for you and your baby. Make a decision that is in harmony with what your body, your baby, and your intuition are telling you. This is truly honoring the mother-baby bond.

Today's mother is bombarded by technology, an endless array of choices, and a medical community that has yet to recognize and honor the mother-baby bond. Doulas can advocate for the mother-baby bond by reminding their clients that it is possible for every mother to tune in to the miracle happening inside her.

The Doula's Action Plan

- Get educated! Learn about the newborn's experience in utero and the unique relationship between the mother and baby during pregnancy.

- Create a marketing plan that attracts mothers early in pregnancy for your doula business. Doulas should encourage a relationship with their clients early in pregnancy. Consider offering early prenatal classes that focus on the mother-baby bond.

- Be mindful of your doula influence and embrace in-person connection early and often throughout the pregnancy. Put your smart phone away and have heart-to-heart communication.

References

Hobel, C, & Culhane, J. (2003). Role of psychosocial and nutritional stress on poor pregnancy outcome. *J Nutr, 133*(5 Supple2): 1709S-1717S.

Marsch, R., Gerber, A.J., & Peterson, B.S. (2008). Neuroimaging studies of normal brain development and their relevance for understanding childhood neuropsychiatric disorders. *Journal of the American Academy of Child and Adolescent Psychiatry, 47*(11), 1233-1251.

O'Rahilly, R., & Mueller, F. (2008). Significant features in the early prenatal development of the human brain. *Annals of Anatomy, 190*, 105-118.

Simmons, R. (2011). Epigenetics and maternal nutrition: nature v. nurture. *Proc Nutr Soc*, *70*(1), 73-81.

Wilson, L., & Wilson Peters, T. (2012). *The greatest pregnancy ever: Keys to the mother-baby bond.* Twin Lakes, WI: Lotus Life Press. (Conscious Agreement is a copyrighted concept within the book. Used in this article with permission.)

Wilson, L., & Wilson Peters, T. (2014). *The attachment pregnancy: The ultimate guide to bonding with your baby.* Fort Collins, CO: Adams Media.

• • • • • •

Laurel Wilson, IBCLC, CLE, CCCE, CLD, and Tracy Wilson Peters, CLE, CCCE, CLD, have more than 40 years of combined experience as pregnancy experts who support mothers and the professionals who work with new families. Their best selling books, *The Attachment Pregnancy: The Ultimate Guide to Bonding with Your Baby* and *The Greatest Pregnancy Ever: Keys to the Mother-baby Bond* unite evidence-based information with heart and mind science to give mothers the tools they need to feel deeply connected to their pregnancies and their

**Laurel Wilson
and Tracy Wilson Peters**

Used with permission.

babies. Additionally, they offer BOND University, which trains perinatal professionals to enhance the bond during pregnancy.

Chapter 3

Supporting a Birthing Woman's Religious or Spiritual Practice

Amy Wright Glenn, MA, CD (DONA)

Who or what created this breathtakingly vast universe? Has it always been? Think of gorgeous galaxies spinning through infinite space. Think of our earth and its diverse expression of life. Questions that are philosophical, religious, or spiritual percolate to the surface in our lives when we encounter deep change and deep mystery. Such questions often come alive for women during pregnancy.

What is religion? To paraphrase Professor Jonathan Z. Smith at the University of Chicago, religions are systems of beliefs and practices that connect us to superhuman beings, powers, or states of mind. Religions have histories and governing bodies and are comprised of institutions with unique traditions. Religious women often turn to a superhuman source and the power of religious tradition, as they draw upon beliefs and practices that sustain them in labor and delivery.

What is spirituality? Spirituality also consists of beliefs and practices that connect people to superhuman beings, powers, or states of mind. While these beliefs and practices may correspond with religious systems, often they are uniquely independent of them. Spiritual people frequently study many traditions, as they craft their own beliefs and personal practices. Spiritual women draw upon their individual approaches to understanding the sacred, which offer strength and comfort through the trials of labor and delivery.

How can doulas best support a birthing woman's religious or spiritual practice? So much of contemporary doula training consists of mastering proven comfort measures for the body and mind. We are trained to offer our best to ease the physical pain of labor. We offer loving and empathetic connection to women as they traverse labor's emotional ups and downs. We acknowledge the benefits of sounding through labor. We know about the use of breath for release and restoration. We encourage women to expand their vision of reality to make room for the intense sensations at hand.

But what about the spirit? The majority of women we work with have a religious or spiritual practice. How can doulas be more effective in acknowledging a woman's unique understanding of the powerful and significant spiritual and/or religious dimensions of birth? How can doulas be more effective in supporting women when it comes to drawing upon a strength that transcends human understanding?

So many of the postures we use as doulas involve coming to the knees to rock through contractions, to help ease lower back pain or to birth. Labor brings women to their knees physically, emotionally, and often spiritually. For women of faith, prayer, meditation, chanting, or the use of sacred imagery emerge naturally in labor. Such heartfelt practices are often vital sources of strength in birth. We will be much more powerful in our ability to comfort and embolden birthing women when we link our repertoire of best practices to supporting a birthing woman's spiritual or religious identity.

I speak from experience. The birth of my son was the most challenging and wonderful event of my life. I prayed. I meditated. I did yoga. I cried. I thought of women who inspired me. I created birth art. My midwives and my doula wanted to know about the details of my spiritual life. This information helped them fully support me in birth.

For example, during a prenatal conversation, I asked my doula to repeat the phrase "All will be well" to me during my labor. I love the mystical writings of Saint Julian of Norwich, and this phrase attributed to her has brought me great peace. I wanted to have my doula say this phrase to me when I couldn't say it myself. So, like an expert gardener, my doula planted the seeds of this calming phrase into my mind when I needed it most. I have vivid memories of her singular voice moving clearly and calmly across the chaos of contractions. "All will be well, Amy. All will be well."

Yet, it is not my own birth story alone that reveals the need for doulas to be mindful and informed of a birthing woman's religious or spiritual identity. The following vignettes also make the point clear.

In Hinduism, repetitive phrases or mantras are used in worship. I've worked with Hindu couples as they draw upon devotional chanting through the labor experience. I once chanted "Om" with a woman in labor for hours. She had the calmest and most natural transition to 10 cm I have ever seen.

Mindfulness of breath is central to many techniques in Buddhist meditation. Indeed, the capacity to stay mindfully present even in the midst of life's turmoil is foundational to Buddhist practice. Some clients I've worked with bring years of meditation practice to their birth experiences. It has been very helpful to remind them of the wonders of breath awareness at critical points in labor.

Through the image of the crucified Jesus and the risen Christ, Christian women have a powerful metaphor of suffering transforming into victory. For Catholic women, images of saints can be very inspiring. I had a Catholic woman once ask me to remind her of Saint Sebastian if she ever felt like giving up. So I did. As she began to spiral into despair at a crucible moment of transition, I calmly looked at her. I held her hands and said, "Saint Sebastian." The transformation was incredible. This image helped her garner the strength needed for a successful vaginal birth after cesarean (VBAC).

In Islam, God is understood as a transcending, yet imminent power. The Qur'an teaches that God is nearer to a person than the jugular vein in the neck. I remember supporting a Muslim couple through the birth of their third child. As the husband lovingly held and slowly danced with his laboring wife, he whispered beloved phrases from the Qur'an into her ear. She wept with the powerful elixir of both beauty and pain. These sacred prayers provide the courage needed to move forward with the birth.

In labor, images of the divine feminine can be meaningful across religious traditions. Images of powerful female goddesses, bodhisattvas, or saints can be very helpful while birthing. For many women artwork focusing on the divine feminine is a wonderful way to internalize the strength and grace embodied in these images in preparation for labor. I've worked with women who draw strength from their understanding of the Goddess. As these women move from maiden to mother, they visualize the powerful legacy of feminine sacred energy that moves through the body in birth.

Amy Wright Glenn

Used with permission.

Clearly, spiritual and religious practices brought into the birth experience are vibrant sources of strength for birthing women. As doulas, there is much more we can do to fully support the religious and/or spiritual component of a birthing woman's identity. Indeed, offering an open-hearted and loving encouragement for such expression needs to be central to the training we receive.

This will require that we look within and examine the implications of our own worldview. How do we interpret the religious or spiritual practices of women, especially when these practices differ from our own understanding of reality? Let's say I'm an atheist and I'm working with a Jewish woman. Or I'm Christian and I have a Muslim client. How do I interpret her system of beliefs and practices?

According to Harvard Professor Diana Eck, there are three main attitudes I can bring to the table. An exclusivist attitude says that my religion, tradition, or point of view is right and others are flawed. An inclusivist point of view says that my religion, tradition, or point of view is right. Yet, other traditions have some truth, and I affirm them to the extent they resonate with my own. The pluralist approach argues that truth - called by many names - transcends all religious or spiritual philosophies. For the pluralist, all ethical paths serve as a means to be able to access the sacred truth of life that is beyond human description. Therefore, another woman's path is held with equal regard to one's own.

Does it matter if a doula is an exclusivist, inclusivist, or pluralist? It should not. Of course, on rare occasions, a doula may decline working with a couple if she finds their metaphysical interpretations of reality an affront to her own. Ideally, however, when it comes to offering excellent spiritual support to a birthing mother, our own understanding of the sacred dimensions of life shouldn't interfere with our capacity to support a birthing woman's approach.

My academic background is in the study of comparative religion and philosophy. For nearly 15 years, I've taught courses in this field. Because of my training, I feel very comfortable in prenatal conversations to ask if a woman has a religious or spiritual practice. I want to be able to support this vital dimension of a birthing woman's identity as a doula.

The first step in offering such support rests in earning the trust of our clients. We earn trust by holding sacred and non-judgmental space. The key to holding sacred space is listening. Yes, we should listen compassionately to her story, her hopes, and her fears, but we must do more than this. We need to also inquire about the beliefs and practices that sustain her soul as she prepares for birth. If inspired and invited, we may even join her in these practices - be it meditation or prayer.

As you meet with your next client in a prenatal conversation, ask if she has a religious or spiritual practice. Let us ask women about the images they have already associated with strength and inspiration. Let us ask women about the sacred and unique practices that work to open their hearts and minds in times of challenge. Reminding women of these images and supporting their religious or spiritual practices are remarkable gifts we can bring to the birth experience.

Indeed, in labor's crucible moments, we can hold these gifts up as we would a mirror. She can look into this reflection and lean into a strength greater than human comprehension. For surely we all want women to be affirmed in their primal - and spiritual - strength as they birth the next generation with great love.

· · · · · ·

Amy Wright Glenn earned her MA in Religion and Education from Teachers College, Columbia University. She taught for 11 years in the Religion and Philosophy Department at The Lawrenceville School in New Jersey, earning the Dunbar Abston Jr. Chair for Teaching Excellence.

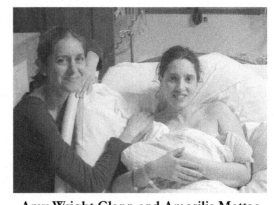

Amy Wright Glenn and Amarilis Matteo

Photo by Kathryn Kruger.
Used with permission.

Amy is a Kripalu Yoga teacher, prenatal yoga teacher, (CD) DONA birth doula, and hospital chaplain. She is the voice for "Motherhood, Spirituality, and Religion" for Philly.com and blogs for Attachment Parenting International, Doula Trainings International, and The Birthing Site. Amy is a regular columnist for Holistic Parenting Magazine and recently published her first book: *Birth, Breath, and Death: Meditations on Motherhood, Chaplaincy, and Life as a Doula.*

Amy teaches private meditation classes via Skype to students across the United States. She also teaches prenatal yoga classes, Mommy and Me Yoga classes, and Breath and Movement Birth Preparation workshops in South Florida.

Chapter 4

How is Being a Doula for Traditionally Observant Jewish Families Different from Working with Other Families?

Amy Mager, MS, LicAc

When a doula is working with a traditionally observant Jewish family, it is helpful for her to become familiar with pertinent aspects of *halakha*, or Jewish law, related to birth and postpartum care. Because there are different interpretations, each family may be different in how they follow the laws. You may want to create a notebook for each family you serve, with a question at the top of the page and room for the answer or answers, as things may change on the rest of the page.

For starters, traditionally observant Jewish women are intimate with their husbands for approximately two weeks out of every month, and do not physically touch them for the rest of the month. The English translation of this concept in Jewish law is "family purity." I prefer to describe it as "keeping intimacy holy with your husband." From the time a woman gets her period, to the time she immerses in a ritual bath or *mikvah*, physical contact between husband and wife is prohibited. At this time, she is called *niddah*. Traditionally, this is a time to build intimacy every month without physical touch and is meant to strengthen the emotional and spiritual components of one's marriage.

As labor progresses, when the time comes that a woman either has a bloody show or has contractions so strong that she can no longer walk, she is niddah and unavailable to her husband for physical touch. Remember how each family is different. The couple may want to discuss this with you together, or the mom may want to speak about this with you woman to woman. This time can be especially challenging for some women in labor, because they do not touch their husbands. Here your presence, loving kindness, and awareness will make a huge difference to the mom you are working with in ways she may be unable to articulate.

Some doulas like to bring snacks for the parents. These parents will keep kosher, following Jewish dietary laws. This means that some families will want to eat only food that they bring, so it's a concern crossed off their list. Other families will go over with you foods and brands they eat. Anything in a package will need to have a sign called a *heksher* designating the rabbi or organization that certifies the item is kosher. Each family has different standards they follow. Know that uncut fresh fruits and vegetables are not an issue.

On *Shabbat*, the Jewish Sabbath, which begins 18 minutes before sundown on Friday evening and goes for roughly 25 hours until Saturday night, everything is different. On Shabbat, traditionally observant Jews will not, under ordinary circumstances, turn lights on and off, cook, enter elevators, or use items that require electricity, or even touch those items. This is another area where there is great diversity in practice, so talk to the family about how they observe and how they would like to deal with potential Shabbat issues that may arise. One way this may come into play is transporting mom and dad to the hospital. This will be addressed by the parents; the doula is not responsible for this. The parents may make arrangements with a cab company in advance; they may choose to leave the car running and locked; or they may make prior arrangements with hospital staff. It's another conversation for your list. When mom is in active labor, any doula can help dad with food for mom, electric doors, lights, and hot packs, for example, although he may not ask directly.

When a laboring woman is in need of anything, it is a *mitzvah*, positive commandment, to prepare it for her, since a woman in childbirth is considered in potential danger. The mitzvah of *pikuach nefesh*, saving a life, takes precedence over the laws of Shabbat, according to halakhah or Jewish law. All of this even further emphasizes the miracle of birth. In the event that there are only Jews present, it is incumbent upon providers to attend to mom's every need AND comfort. In an emergency, whoever is there is required to do whatever it takes to meet mom's physical and emotional needs. When the doula is Jewish, whether she is a practicing Jew or not, because she IS Jewish by Jewish law, the mom may not ask the doula to do things she can live without. This is a conversation a non-practicing Jewish doula would want to have prenatally.

Some hospitals in areas with large Jewish populations have a Shabbat elevator, which stops on every floor. Understand that if someone's life is not in danger, and she is a traditionally observant Jew, she would not get in the elevator, but would use the stairs. If walking is not possible, some husbands will get into the elevator with their wives to support them. Others will walk up the stairs knowing that you are present and supportive of mom. Some hospitals have a Shabbat hospitality room with pre-made food for use by anyone in need on Shabbat. Ask ahead of time. Typically, these rooms have a code that is written in Hebrew, so those in the "know" can gain access.

Many traditionally observant Jewish women cover their hair, although not all. Some women may cover their hair, except when they are alone with their husbands. Some will cover their hair just at *shul*, in a house of prayer; others when they leave their own home; and others cover their hair all the time. For some women, concern about having to pull on a headscarf can be a distraction to being present and able to focus on her contractions in labor. If that becomes an issue, you can remind mom that you can take on making sure her hair is covered in a compassionate, loving manner, so she can focus on the task at hand.

As a doula, know that your observant Jewish mom may need lots of hands on, loving, compassionate care from you in ways that dad may provide at other births. When dad is in the room, he will, hopefully, be loving and present with mom. Some dads may stand in the corner saying *Tehillim*, or psalms. The purpose is to put an intentional, spiritual protection around the mom and baby, praying for a birth with ease, a healthy baby, and a complete recovery. Some moms also choose to say tehillim while they are in labor. Birth is the space between life and death; therefore, the heavens open up for the family and they may ask the Creator for anything. After baby is born, mom will say prayers thanking God for the birth of her baby.

Different families have different practices, and some may have permission from their rabbi to do things a certain way. Please do not be shy and DO ask questions. A loving, kind, compassionate presence is the most important requirement.

If women get stuck, I encourage them to connect with and talk to their precious one. I ask mom to remind the baby that this is the first of many times they will work together as a team. Ask mom to remember that this precious baby has been preparing for this journey and will be born *B'sha'a tova*, in the perfect hour. Reminding moms that birth is a normal process, that women are strong, and that our bodies were designed to birth is your job. Sometimes the work is about the DOING - the act of massage, breathing with mom, encouraging dad to look into her eyes and breathe with her. Sometimes it is about BEING - using a quiet, loving, kind presence and believing with every fiber of our being in mom's ability to birth.

An important piece of wisdom that was passed on to me before my first birth is from the work of Adele Faber and Elaine Mazlish. Their book *How to Talk So Kids Will Listen and Listen So Kids Will Talk* changes how parents will move forward after the birth. I believe this book should be given to all parents when they get pregnant, so they can work on these skills when their babies are inside. This way they will have the tools in mind and mouth as their children grow. What they teach is in line with traditionally observant Judaism, that we need to teach each child according to her nature.

Knowing and understanding the needs of each particular family will be vital for a successful experience. What makes working with traditionally observant Jewish moms different from working with other moms who are giving birth? What looks like a whole lot of rules from the outside is a blueprint for this community regarding how they live their spiritual lives on the inside. The goal for these families is to elevate daily tasks and common, mundane experiences to make them holy, to provide meaning. With this information, you, as their doula, can facilitate your understanding of what brings ease, which will go a long way towards a birth that meaningfully supports the new family.

• • • • • •

Amy Mager MS, LicAc, apprenticed for two years with Raven Lang, OMD, midwife, and acupuncturist. Amy studied extensively with Dr. Miriam Lee, highly respected acupuncturist and author. She has been published in the book *Parenting from the Heart* and the magazines "Natural Jewish Parenting" and "Stepping Stones."

Amy Mager

Photo by Sarah Prall.
Used with permission.

Her eight years of professional education include a four-year MS program at the American College of Traditional Chinese Medicine and a degree from the Post-Graduate Institute of Oriental Medicine in Hong Kong. She became a birth educator and birth assistant through Informed Birth and Parenting. Amy is a trained lactation counselor and has worked with nursing women for 22 years. She continues to expand her knowledge through continuing education and her work with patients.

Amy lives in Springfield, Massachusetts, with her husband Dan Garfield, D.C. She has birthed six children, nursed for 16 years, and is grateful for each of her precious ones. She can be reached at 413.222.8616 or AmyMagerHealing@gmail.com.

Chapter 5

Honoring the Sacred and Cultivating Ritual

Kristen Avonti, Birth Keeper

The journey of a mother through conception, pregnancy, birthing, and embracing life with a newborn is deeply and richly built upon a sacred relationship with her own inner awareness and her capacity to create a new life. Throughout all of history, this time within a woman's life has been filled with the creation of sacred rituals and rites of passage for each new mother.

Today, these rituals and ceremonial initiations into motherhood still exist, even if we don't often conceive of them as such. For many new moms, their rituals of pregnancy are centered around their experiences in the medicalized paradigm of pregnancy and birth. They eagerly await their 20-week ultrasound to find out the gender of the baby. For many, the progression from monthly to bi-weekly to weekly doctor's appointments marks the journey of pregnancy. Baby showers filled with quaint rituals, games, and elaborate cakes are the norm among many social circles. Filling a nursery with all of the "essentials" (and often many non-essentials as well!) quells the nesting urge and warms many mothers' hearts. For many moms the socially constructed pregnancy rituals are some of the aspects most adored during the pregnancy journey.

But for others, these rituals leave something to be desired. As we, a culture of strong and embodied women, begin to reclaim the sacred nature of birthing, many of us are beginning to seek and desire a paradigm of pregnancy and birthing. We want one that honors the deeply intimate inner journey that guides us from womanhood into motherhood, regardless of whether we are birthing our first baby or our fifth.

Women have begun to seek out a new paradigm to support their pregnancy and birthing journeys. We have begun to honor the sacred nature of this time of total transformation, surrender, growth, and becoming. We are turning to our midwives and our doulas, our sisters, friends, and communities to support us in creating new rituals that can hold and support this incredible journey. So often we find ourselves carving this path we wish to walk upon; at times, bushwhacking our way through the forest of culturally ingrained ideals about what it means to be pregnant or give birth in an attempt to rediscover and remember what it is to birth in a way that honors the sacred nature of this time within our lives.

Conscious Conception:
A New Beginning

What would it be like if all new life began within the container of a conscious conception? What if a woman was supported in consciously calling in the essential spirit and essence of a being perfectly aligned for her and her family constellation? What if she knew the moment she conceived? What if conception was an act of true soul union - the joining of two beings in the creation of one new life form?

Within the green world of our herbal allies, Partridgeberry, *Mitchella repens*, stands as the guardian of our conscious conception. A low-lying, shade-loving, woodland plant, two trumpet-shaped flowers erupt from the small, glossy, green leaves. Although each flower within the pair embodies both the female and male reproductive parts of the plant, one is more strongly present in its female anatomy, while the other is more strongly masculine. Together the two flowers join in the formation of one single berry, the union of their sacred connection. As the berry ripens, the flowers slowly fade away, leaving a bright, red, plump berry with two indentations, which bear the mark of the flowers from which it was birthed. In the sacred union of the plant world, two join in the creation of one perfect fruit - a beautiful parallel for the sacred union of two souls in the conception of a consciously conceived being. It's no surprise that on the physiological plane, Partridgeberry is a female tonic for all aspects of the reproductive system, but most specifically as a uterine and fertility tonic, as well as what is known as a "partus preparatory," or an herb which prepares the uterus for childbirth. Through cultivating a relationship with this plant on the physical, spiritual, and energetic planes of existence, we can begin to call into our awareness the subtleties of consciously conceiving.

For many couples or women journeying through pregnancy, the concept of a conscious conception has never entered their purview of reality. The idea that we can consciously call forth the qualities and energies of the soul we birth into being has yet to become part of our collective conscious awareness. Some mothers or parents may deeply desire this quality of sacredness and ceremony within their pregnancy, but feel unsure how to enact it within their lives. Many women have had the experience of knowing the energetic qualities or even personalities of their children before conception or while their children were still in the womb. I have spoken to women who are pregnant or in the flow of new motherhood, who have shared with me that this being they have birthed has been traveling with them throughout the entirety of their life, awaiting the perfect moment to be born. In some cultures a child's conception is believed to occur the moment the being was a thought within his or her mother's awareness. It is from that moment forward that she has been carrying him or her within her being.

Sometimes physical conception takes time; sometimes it happens immediately. Sometimes that being is already perfectly formed, and other times it must travel for a period of time, strengthening the bonds of those soul contracts before manifesting into physical form. Many traditions honor and hold that a child chooses the family into which it will be born based on the karmic journey of this life's path. In the divine unfolding of all that is held within the universe, a child chooses its mother specifically because they each possess the love, wisdom, grace, and life lessons the other needs. They are the cosmic pairing and karmic unfolding of a path of mutual destiny. Within this paradigm there is an invitation to invite in consciously and with clarity the willingness to embrace that relationship of perfect alignment. Through the co-creation of sacred ceremony and a deeply personal ritual, we cultivate the capacity to be fully present from the moment of conception, with this new earth being we will birth.

Creating a Conscious Conception Ceremony with Your Clients

Each mother or couple will have their own ideas and ideals regarding what feelings resonate for them as individuals and as a family unit. It is our job, as a sacred companion in this process, to hold space for whatever feels most aligned for each family. Some couples or women may have a very clear sense of how they wish to create a ritual for the conscious conception of their child. Others may have never even heard of the practice, but feel enticed by the opportunity to engage consciously with the emergence of this new being. Some may have been trying to conceive for a long time and hope that creating ceremony and ritual may aid their endeavors. Others may have already conceived, intentionally or unintentionally, and may desire to utilize this opportunity to welcome and bless this new life that is already growing within them. This may be her very first pregnancy, or perhaps she knows it will be the one that completes her family. She may be in the process of still healing from a previous loss or may be embarking on this journey within the context of a deep spiritual or religious practice. In whatever way your client has chosen to greet this process, begin by engaging her in a dialogue about what she most deeply desires through this ritual or ceremony.

Create a space that is conducive to tapping into the deepest places of our inner awareness. Calling in a new life is a deeply profound and sacred journey, one which often requires us to soften our walls and open to our own vulnerability. A conscious conception ceremony can take place in your client's home, in your office, or in any space that feels sacred to your client. You may wish to set up an altar with items that are sentimental to your client, represent their family unit, or are symbolic of conception, pregnancy, birth, or family. You may wish to light some candles and burn some incense or sage. You and your client may wish to have soft music playing in the background, you may prefer silence, or you may simply want to enjoy the sounds of nature. You may wish to begin with a moment of centering and meditation to bring your awareness into the present moment and the deeply sacred nature of the ritual you are embarking upon. If it resonates for you, you may wish to open sacred space, according to whatever tradition you and your clients are most aligned. This may involve calling in the directions and the elements or offering a prayer to the spiritual allies or higher power with whom you and/or your clients resonate.

The opportunity to facilitate a conscious conception ceremony is a deep honor and loving act of service. Your role is to serve as a guide through this journey into the depths of their souls and to support them in calling in the soul threads of this new life. Begin by inviting your clients to imagine their family unit as it is currently manifested. Perhaps this is their first baby, and it is just the mother and her partner. Perhaps you are working with a woman choosing to enter into motherhood on her own. Or perhaps her family is already very full. Invite her to imagine what it is that she loves most about her family as it is currently constructed:

- What qualities best describe you as a family and the love you share?

- What values, ideals, and principles define you as a family or the family you wish to create?

Allow her to fully sink into her own inner awareness of the qualities that define her family. Create space for both mother and her partner, if present, to envision and share the qualities that are most important to them as individuals and as a family unit:

- Now, bring your awareness to your desire to grow your family. What do you wish to cultivate within your family unit through the addition of a new member?

- How will this new child complement the love you already share and hold?

- What gifts will this new baby bring into your family?

- How will he or she fill you and complete you?

Invite her, and her partner if present, to envision the qualities they hope to cultivate within their child:

- What values do you hope to cultivate or instill within this new life?

- What qualities or traits will add to or complement your family structure?

- What are your dreams or visions for the life this child will live?

It can be helpful to support your clients in being
in selecting just the right word or phrase to truly a
deepest desires. A conscious conception is an oppor
with one's highest alignment and manifest a being who
tune with the matrix of one's family. Sometimes it can tak
to really get to the heart of a desire or vision and articulate
precise wording possible. When the mother, or her partner, fin
or phrase that articulates her deepest vision or desire, invite her t
it on her piece of paper. As the vision continues to build and gain c
support the couple in holding this vision and imagining what this bud
new life may be like. It is important to remember throughout this proces
that we are planting seeds of intention, rather than attaching ourselves
to a specific idea or vision. Above all else, this ritual is an opportunity to
express gratitude for the opportunity to conceive, carry, and birth this
new life into being.

Once this process feels complete, you can invite your clients to explore
their vision through other non-verbal forms of expression. Drawing,
painting, or creating a clay sculpture can be a beautiful way to express
that which often cannot be captured in words. These images or sculpted
objects can be displayed or placed on a pregnancy altar as a reminder of
the love and intention which brought this child into the world.

Some women may choose to also create a private ceremony for her and
her partner during the time of actual conception. Counseling a woman
on tools to track her fertility can empower her and her partner to time
their love-making, so they may be consciously present in sacred space
for the time when sperm and egg have the opportunity to unite. Other
women, however, may benefit from taking a moment at the close of
their conscious conception ceremony to surrender to the divine timing
of conception. For many women, it is in the act of total surrender and
letting go of the desire to control the timing and outcome of their
conception that the divine union can result in the creation of a new life.
It is often nice to offer a small gift, such as a candle, that can be lit by
the couple anytime they wish to remember the flame which was ignited
during this sacred and special ritual or which can be re-lit while they make
love to conceive or during the birth.

The Sacred Nature of Pregnancy

The journey of pregnancy is an invitation to step deeply into the
transformative process of peeling away the layers and exploring our
innermost places of healing, growth, and expansion. As we move
through the various phases and stages of pregnancy, labor, and birth,
we are invited to expand our conscious awareness and physical form in
the creation of a new life. So often it feels beyond the grasp of words to
describe what it feels like to grow a second heart out of your blood, out

ɔnstruct a human being, to carry
ʋomb, in the cauldron of your
bout the journey from woman
ɡrasp of words, so life changing.]
me consumed by the day to day,
ɪur life, and the taxing toll that
and almost expected that we will
ɪsy that come with creating a

43

t learning to be present in
ɪure of exactly what it is. To
ɪtation, in becoming. Whether
ɪ want to or not. My heart is growing larger.
ɪMy capacity to love is growing deeper. I am open from my Crown to
my Root. I open to the world and the essential nature of all that is. I am
pouring in nutrients, nourishment, and life force from the mother of
all, funneling in the energetic threads, which are being woven into the
tapestry of a soul." Day by day, the threads collect, weaving the unique
matrix which will inform this child's entire being. You are a vessel, a
cauldron of creation and gestation. You are housing an incredible being,
who is being formed, cell by cell, neuron by neuron by the very nature
of your existence. Moments of connection streaming together to form a
soul, a consciousness, an entire lifetime.

This journey of pregnancy is an opportunity to slow the speed of your
inner life, to succumb to swirling in the portal of pregnancy. It seems as
though the moment we conceive something shifts within the subtleties
of our brains or the energetic make up of our entire being. Our thinking
begins to slow, our dreams become more vivid, and everything around
us seems to be painted in a different hue. That sideways glance from a
stranger seems to crumple your self-esteem. The snarky comment your
partner always makes, now suddenly strikes a chord that can send you
to tears. The newest Hallmark commercial, your favorite love song, and
the romantic drama you rented on Netflix - all are equally tear inducing.
Everything is richer, deeper, more vibrant, more saturated.

[Pregnancy is an invitation to allow life to become a living ritual - a time to
carve out space within your inner awareness to embody and embrace the
miracle of pure existence and pure creation, but it requires us to choose
to attune to the sacred. It requires our ongoing commitment to pause in
the hustle and bustle of our daily lives and honor and appreciate the
beauty of the journey we are dancing within.]

Sacred Pregnancy Altars
and Living Rituals

Carving out space within your relationship with your clients can help to cultivate this sense of the sacred within the journey of pregnancy. Beginning prenatal appointments with a few moments of meditation, grounding, or centering can support the active pause required to be present for the inner journey of this time of deep transformation. Inviting a woman to see the sacred in her day-to-day experiences and tap into her inner awareness of the self-evident beauty of life, can plant the seeds of living consciously in all that she experiences.

Creating a pregnancy altar is a tangible tool that can support mothers and their partners in remembering the sacred nature of this journey. An altar can be as simple as a small space on a windowsill or on top of a dresser where sentimental and meaningful objects are placed as a reminder of the great joy and gratitude of carrying a new life within. Or they can be elaborate and ornate centerpieces which feature prominently in one's living space and create a dynamic energetic presence. However your clients choose to cultivate or construct their altars, it should reflect and embody the aspects of growing a family which are most meaningful to them as individuals.

Taking time daily, weekly, or as the mood may strike to be present with their altars and reflect on their experiential journey of being and becoming can invite the sacred into their day-to-day lives and help them to cultivate a sense of living ritual within their lives. Learning to embrace this journey as a living ritual and expression of one's most profound capacities for growth and creation is a gift that can support a mother on all levels of her being. Being present to honor the journey, in all of its messy reality, with its roller coaster ride of ups and downs, is the living practice of the art of living consciously. Through your relationship with your clients you have a wondrous opportunity to support the cultivation of living rituals of connection and embodiment through simple guided meditations and inviting a dialogue into the sacred heart of the journey of pregnancy.

Mother Blessing: A Ritual of Honoring

A Mother Blessing ritual, sometimes referred to as a "Blessingway," is a tradition of creating a sacred space to honor a woman in the time just before she is to give birth. A blessingway originates from an age-old Native American tradition which honors the times of deep transformation in an individual's life. Although many continue to refer to Mother Blessing ceremonies as a "Blessingway," some wonder whether we are appropriating a tradition that is not truly ours to own. As a result, the term "Mother Blessing" has arisen as an appropriate reference to the true nature of this beautiful ritual.

A Mother Blessing can take many forms and should be ideally suited to meet each individual mother where she is, honoring the aspects of celebration, ritual, and ceremony that are most meaningful to her. Some women choose to blend the culturally common practice of having a baby shower with the more intimate ideals of a Mother Blessing. Others choose to veer entirely from the cultural norm of a baby shower and embrace a deeply spiritual ritual centered around their time of transition. Most, however, find a middle ground between the two, which blends the unique aspects that support her as an individual woman in a time of deep transition and transformation.

A Mother Blessing is a time to gather and embrace becoming a mother in a circle of love, support, and nourishment. Most often these circles include just women and may be comprised of a woman's close family, her friends, or a combination of the two. Sometimes, however, a woman may choose to invite her partner into the circle or her male relatives as well. Truly, this time is about serving her individual needs, regardless of pre-existing customs. As we transition into a culture which holds and supports our mothers in a new paradigm of health and healing, we can support the co-creation of this time of profound nourishment, support, and healing. Many women don't realize this deep level of honoring and support is available to them, and many who do realize it is something they desire feel they must create it for themselves. Being able to soften into a state of receptivity is a deeply nourishing act of both self-care and allowing oneself to be supported by one's community. As doulas, midwives, sisters, and friends, we hold a valuable role in co-creating a new norm of caring for our women.

Crafting a Mother Blessing

The co-creation and facilitation of a Mother Blessing ritual begins by engaging a mother-to-be in a deep, heart-to-heart conversation about what her deepest desires are for this time of in-between, softening, and transition. How can her community, her friends, her sisters, and her family most deeply nourish and support her? What would be most meaningful to HER as an individual woman about to enter into the portals of transformation held within her birthing time? Sometimes it can help to have a list of ideas to explore with the mother-to-be, especially in this time when many women have never heard of or attended a Mother Blessing. Some women, however, will already have clear ideas about what they wish to incorporate or include within the ceremony. Each Mother Blessing ritual will be tailored to the specific interests, desires, and needs of the woman who is receiving the blessing. Some rituals may be more mainstream and may even include traditional baby shower style gift giving, particularly if it is a woman's first pregnancy and there is a lot she needs in preparation for this baby. Other women may choose to have two separate celebrations, one to focus on the spiritual support and nourishment and the other structured more akin to a traditional baby shower. Women with a deep spiritual or religious practice may also wish to include aspects of their spirituality that are most meaningful to them into this time of honoring and celebration.

You may wish to offer or include any of the following:

- **Nourishing Foods** - Fill a buffet table with mother's favorite comfort foods, along with fresh fruit, chocolate, nourishing snacks, or a full meal, and nourishing infusions of Red Raspberry leaf, Nettles, or Oatstraw.

- **Meal Train** - Invite guests to bring a freezer-friendly meal that the mother-to-be can bring home and store for the postpartum time.

- **Altar Building** - Create an altar for the ritual. Begin by laying down a decorative cloth. Add candles, fresh flowers, and symbols of pregnancy, birth, mothering, and the divine feminine. Invite guests to bring items to add to the altar, such as sentimental

Mother blessing altar

Photo by Kristen Avonti.
Used with permission.

objects, stones, crystals, shells, feathers, small art items, or other objects which are beautiful or meaningful. At the close of the ritual, pack up the altar items for the woman to take home and create a pregnancy or birth altar.

- **Opening Circle** - Open sacred space with a prayer, meditation, or by calling in the elements and directions.

- **Name Honoring** - As each guest introduces herself, invite her to share how she knows the woman being honored and also invite her to share her maternal relations. For example, "I am Kristen, mother of Jensen, Elijah, and Amelia., daughter of Carol, granddaughter of Judith and Marion."

- **Weaving the Web** - Beginning with the mother-to-be, use a ball of yarn, hemp string, or cordage to wrap around each attendant's wrist. As the cord is wrapped, invite the women to offer a prayer or intention for the mother or her birth. When the circle is complete, the cord is cut and tied around each attendant's wrist. These bracelets are left on as a reminder of the energy being held for this mother and her birth until after the baby is born, and serves as a reminder for the mother-to-be of the circle of women who support her.

- **Foot Bathing** - Prepare an herbal footbath, with warm water, fresh flower petals or dried herbs, sea salt, and essential oils. Allow the mother to soak her feet while sitting in the circle, being massaged and enjoying nourishing treats, or being surrounded by song.

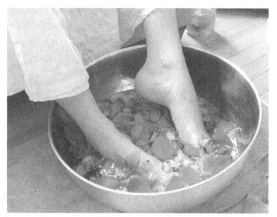

Foot bath

Photo by Kristen Avonti.
Used with permission.

- **Massage** - Offer the woman a nourishing massage on her hands, feet, legs, belly, wherever she may be comfortable. Use a nourishing oil, such as sesame, almond or jojoba, and add a few drops of essential oil, such as lavender or rose.

- **Pampering** - Some women enjoy having their hair brushed or braided or receiving a manicure or pedicure during their Mother Blessing.

- **Belly Art** - Adorn the mother's belly with beautiful art in the form of body paint, henna, or a belly cast.

- **Quilt Squares** - Have an art station set up with supplies for women to decorate squares of fabric which can be sewn together into a beautiful quilt for the mother or baby.

- **Prayer Flags** - Using squares or pendants of fabric, fabric markers, paint, or other art supplies for creating images, invite women to create empowering prayer flags which can be hung in the birthing space.

- **Clay Sculpting** - Gather ready-to-bake clay and invite the women present to sculpt images which remind them of pregnancy, birth, mothering, beauty, nature, or the strength of the woman being honored. Reserve enough time to bake these items before the close of the ceremony, usually 30 minutes, depending on the type of clay chosen and the thickness of the object. The mother-to-be can then take these objects home and add them to her birth altar.

- **Birth Affirmations** - Invite women to make note cards or small pictures which can be hung around the home or in the birthing space which include words of strength, empowerment, and inspiration.

- **Intention Setting** - Invite each woman to share her prayers and intentions for the mother-to-be, the birth, or her baby. It is often helpful to invite guests to write these intentions or blessings down prior to the ritual, so that the mother can refer back to them during the remainder of the pregnancy or birth, or keep them in a keepsake journal.

- **Sharing Birth Stories** - Invite women to share their stories of birth, attending birth, or mothering. It can be such an amazing journey to witness and share the incredible array of experiences we have as women.

- **Blessing Bead Necklace/Bracelet** - Invite each woman who is attending to bring a bead. Have a string or thin cord prepared, as well as a clasp. (Bear in mind that some women may bring beads with very small holes. Choose a string that is sturdy but thin!) Have each woman add her bead and offer a blessing for the mother-to-be.

- **Medicine Making** - Gather herbs, such as comfrey, calendula, rosemary, lavender, witch hazel, rose, yarrow, and St. John's Wort, as well as jars or decorative bags to fill with herbs for a postpartum sitz bath blend. Invite each woman to fill a jar or bag with a combination of the herbs gathered, so that the mother can bring home her collection of ready-to-use sitz bath blends.

- **Luminary Crafting** - Gather tall glass candles, glue or Mod Podge, paint, tissue paper, and images which symbolize birth, beauty, pregnancy, empowerment, strength, and the energy of the woman being honored. You can also have a collection of old magazines from which the women present can cut words or images that call to them. Cover the outer surface of the candle with inspiring, empowering, and beautiful images. Gift these luminaries to the mother-to-be to fill her birthing or home space with inspiring images and love-filled light.

- **Candle Ceremony** - Have a small candle for each attendant to take home with them. Set up a calling tree or email list, and invite the women to light their candles and offer prayers when the mother-to-be goes into labor or has her baby.

- **Singing, Chanting, Music, or Drumming** - Create space within the ritual or ceremony for song or music. Perhaps you wish to prepare some well-loved songs or chants ahead of time, or invite the women attending to think of songs they may wish to share.

- **Pictures** - If the mother wishes, help her to remember and capture her special day with lots of pictures of the day's festivities, her beautiful belly, and the circle of women who have come to support her.

- **Gift Giving** - Invite guests to bring small, sentimental, or practical gifts, which most deeply meet the family's needs.

- **Closing** - Invite the women to gather back in the center of the circle. Offer a song, chant, moment of prayer or meditation, or just an opportunity to hold hands in a circle and offer a group blessing to the mother-to-be.

Honoring the Ritual in it All

As women who serve the community of women entering into and transitioning through pregnancy, birth, and motherhood, we are gifted with the amazing, unique, and beautiful opportunity to serve as the guardians of sacred birthing and the instigators of a new culture of healing. Through the many faces of the work you do with birthing women, you stand at the crossroads of the co-creation of a new paradigm for honoring and holding our birthing and pregnant women. Each moment you share with a mother - before she conceives, as she journeys through pregnancy, during the birth, in the postpartum period, and throughout her life as your relationship continues to develop and grow - you are invited to embrace and embody the sacred in all she is experiencing. As you deepen your relationship to this work, allow yourself to emanate the beauty and presence of ritual in every interaction. Each moment we share with another woman and her growing family is sacred, and when honored and witnessed with our deepest sense of reverence, gratitude, love, and passion, even the seemingly simple moments are transformed into living rituals of healing, love, and transformation.

· · · · · ·

Kristen Avonti is a homesteading mother to four beautiful children, living in the hills of Shutesbury, Massachusetts. She has had a passion for natural living and the plant world since a very young age, growing up in the gardens and the kitchen, working side-by-side with her father. Kristen received her Bachelor of Arts from Hampshire College, with a focus on Psychology and Herbal Medicine. She went on to complete an herbal apprenticeship and birth doula and midwifery education. Her studies have continued through workshops, conferences, online courses, and self-study. Kristen received her Reiki Master-Teacher certification and is studying shamanism on an ongoing basis with her mentor. Currently, Kristen is also studying with Aviva Jill Romm in her Women's Herbal Health Educator program.

Kristen Avonti

Photo by Franesa Pyle.
Used with permission.

Kristin founded Tree of Dreams Sanctuary on her land in Shutesbury, Massachusetts. Tree of Dreams Sanctuary is a holistic healing educational center and healing arts practice dedicated to community and individual healing, education, personal growth, and the preservation of medicinal plants.

Currently, Kristen teaches a variety of workshops, courses, and apprenticeship programs, both on site and throughout New England. She is an adjunct faculty member at the University of Massachusetts, where she teaches courses in shamanism and herbal medicine. In addition, Kristen operates a healing arts practice where she sees clients for herbal consultations, women's health services, pregnancy support, Reiki, and shamanic healing. Kristen's work is fueled by a passion for healing, a dedication to carrying forward the medicine ways, and a deep love and connection with the natural world.

Chapter 6

The Doula's Role in Unexpected Homebirths: Oh My Gosh, She's Pushing!

Teresa Howard, CLD, CLE, BOLD, DFB

You have a client due any day now. She calls you and everything sounds very early - moderate cramping, no bloody show, and erratic contractions she is able to talk through. You remind her to keep hydrated, eat light snacks, and go about her normal daily routine, but stay close to home to rest.

A few hours later, you get a call from her - things are picking up, but she is not feeling ready to move to the birth center or hospital yet. She would like you to come now to be with her and her partner. You listen through a contraction and agree that it is a perfect time for you to come. The contractions are a bit inconsistent, but getting stronger. She is feeling a lot in her back now. You remind her of the positions that will help the most to get the baby aligned perfectly and tell her you are on your way.

You have already showered and readied your birth bag, anticipating this call. You grab your water bottle, and knowing your car is packed, you head out to meet her. When you arrive 45 minutes later, she is moaning loudly and rocking her hips, while her partner is providing comforting backstrokes. She looks up and smiles at seeing your face.

Things have definitely made a quick turn. She has gone from a bit chatty to very serious. The contractions are now three minutes apart and lasting 90 seconds. You ask when she last emptied her bladder, and suggest it may be time to head to the birthplace.

The mom moves slowly to the bathroom and pulls down her pants. You notice a lot of bloody show. Hmmm, rapid dilation? She sits on the toilet and empties her bladder, and immediately begins to involuntarily push. The thought, "Holy crap!" crosses your mind and you begin to pray internally. What do you do?

The first thing I do is ask the mom to put her finger in her vagina and tell me if she feels anything firm, and I look at her perineum to see if it is bulging. Sometimes just the baby moving down can cause a momentary feeling of pressure and first time mothers often push for hours. She tells you she feels something hard right inside. When did her water break? Oh, she thinks maybe when she was in the tub she felt a release. Okay!

The next thing you do is ask the dad to call 911. I have had some couples decline to do so. (The midwives in our area have asked us to call if the parents decline. They can decide to let them in, depending on how they feel at their arrival. You are not a midwife; you are a doula. Although you have tons of experience at births, catching babies is not in your repertoire. In case of an emergency, it would be nice to have the team available if they are needed.)

Ask the couple if they feel they want to move to the birth location, and explain that based on what you are assessing, they could be having a baby roadside. If the mom feels the baby's head, it would probably be safer to stay put at this point.

If they decide to stay, ready the space. Either fill the tub or make a clean, waterproof area for the mom to birth. Remember, babies that come quickly are usually not held up by anything. I have an emergency birth mini manual by Gregory White in my car, along with some gloves, but I have yet to use them. If the partner is present, they can make a wonderful catcher. The 911 dispatcher is usually on the phone on speaker and can guide the partner to birth this baby.

Your job is to doula the couple. Provide a voice of comfort and calm, even though you are spinning inside. If the partner is not willing or not present, keep calm and allow the mom to follow her instincts with you being her support.

If you have a pair of gloves, this is a great time to put them on. If not, wash your hands and remove any rings. Support the mom's perineum with a firm hand, and allow the baby to slowly emerge. Help the mom not to blast her baby out too quickly. Feel as the head emerges to see if there is a cord around the baby's neck. If there is, see if it is loose and hold it a bit away as the baby slips under it. Remind yourself that babies that come quickly are not usually hung up by anything. Stay calm and trust birth.

By this time, you can usually hear the sirens. Sometimes paramedics come busting in and create a huge disturbance, sometimes they enter peacefully and observe until they are needed. There is no rush at this point. They may want to start an IV in case of bleeding. They may want to cut the cord quickly - the parents can ask them to wait. They may want to transport the mother before the placenta arrives. The parents get to decide if this is what they want or if they want to wait to see if it comes on its own.

Some couples decide not to go to the hospital. Your job is not to advise, but to help them gather options. Call the care provider and ask what they would like the couple to consider. Help the mom have skin-to-skin with the baby and breastfeed if she desires, since it is what is best for her and the baby. Keep everyone warm.

Rarely, I have had unplanned catches in the hospital. It happens. When you attend a lot of births (I have doulaed for 577 births), it is going to happen. It is imperative that you have assistance on the way, since sometimes it is needed. Stay calm. Even though inside you are an emotional mess, take a deep breath and trust birth.

My first unplanned catch at a hospital was with a mom who had just been checked and found to be 7 cm. She was told she could get in the tub. She got out of the bed, pushed once, and the baby's head emerged. I got my apprentice to get the nurse. I changed places with the dad and threw a towel on the floor. I held the mom while dad did the catch.

Ironically, I caught her second baby in the tub at the same hospital a few years later. My client's partner was on his way from a job interview. She was in the same room as her first birth and entered the tub at 7 cm again. She was trying to wait until her partner got there, but she put her feet on the floor of the tub in a squat and gave one push. I pulled the cord - I had warned the nurses she goes fast after seven. They arrived to find my hand cradling the crowning head. They could not get in to help her, so they suggested she push again, and I brought her baby up to her chest.

The next catch was also at a hospital. The mom had been 10 cm for at least an hour, with no urge to push. Once she emptied her bladder, the baby presented on the perineum. I called for the nurse who remained in the room. She suggested her partner and I move the mom to the bed, and when she stood up, the baby slid into my hands, as I saved it from hitting the floor.

I once talked to a mom on the phone who was in labor at home by herself, awaiting the arrival of her partner. It was her second baby. It was obvious she was in very active labor. I headed there, but also called her midwife to let her know I did not think she would be coming in. This labor had slipped up on her, as it was her second baby and her first labor had been a long one. She was in denial. I then called a homebirth midwife who was in the area and asked if she could consider coming to meet us. When I pulled into the driveway, I could hear her on the phone pushing. She could feel the baby's head. I asked if I could call 911, she said no. I asked if I could try to get her to the nearest hospital and she declined. Her husband arrived, and they decided to fill up the tub and have their son born there. The dad declined catching, and I supported the mom as her baby was born in the caul. I was so delighted that within minutes the homebirth midwife arrived. They did not go into the hospital at all, but called to chat with their hospital midwife. The homebirth midwife checked out the baby, who went to the pediatrician the next day.

My next catch was for a mom who arrived at the hospital in early labor. She stayed for three hours. Although I thought she gave the appearance of someone in active labor, her cervix remained unchanged. She decided to head home. She declined my repeated offer to go with her and her husband. She kept saying she did not want to be one of those moms who comes to the hospital too early. After I returned home, her husband asked me to come to their home. When I walked into her bathroom, the look on her face told the whole story. I spoke with her midwife and asked if she could stop by their home on the way to the hospital. She agreed. The mom slipped into the tub and birthed her son into her hands and mine within minutes of my arrival. (The dad preferred to be at her head during the birth.) The midwife checked her out after the birth, and then her husband drove her to the hospital to have a small repair done.

I have had moms give birth in cars and at home without me there - quick and without any issues. One mom was supposed to be heading to the hospital when I got a call that before they could get out the door, the baby had been born quickly on her bed. She had gotten in the shower just minutes earlier, since her labor was less than an hour of noticeable contractions. I detoured to their home and was the first one there. The EMTs came very quickly after me. I helped her get her placenta out by suggesting she sit on the toilet with a bag to catch the placenta. This was their second baby, so things had changed quickly. The EMTs were gentle and patient. They stayed until the placenta was out, and her bleeding was minimal. She chose to go to the pediatrician and did not see the midwife in her office until later.

One mom had been having irregular contractions for days. Her baby finally lined up perfectly, and she immediately realized the baby was coming quickly. Originally, she was headed to the hospital, so I went there, but soon the dad called to tell me how, after sitting on the toilet, she stepped into the tub instead. They had called 911. The dispatcher sent EMTs who stood in the doorway of the bathroom as the dad did the catch.

I doulaed a mom who lived very close to the hospital and me. When I arrived, she was in the shower, and all of the sudden needed to give birth. This was her first baby and she had only been in labor for a couple of hours. The EMTs arrived and thought it was a planned homebirth. She was pushing and did not want to leave. They told her she could push for a few contractions, and if the baby was not crowning, they wanted to transport her via ambulance to the hospital. That is what happened. I followed, and she gave birth shortly after arriving at the OB unit.

I talked a dad through the birth of their baby at an intersection where he could see the hospital, but they were stuck in traffic. The mom birthed on the floorboard of the front passenger-side seat. She loved her birth. I met them at the hospital soon after. Another time, I talked a dad through the birth of their baby who came quickly, met them at home, and helped get them to the hospital for the repair that was needed from the quick push.

Birth happens. It happens on its own time and babies come when they want to come. Sometimes there is no pattern of contractions. Often, we think this is something that only happens with a multipara, but nope, it can happen with a primipara, too! Of the four unplanned catches I've done, one mom was birthing her first baby. I have been present for a first-time mom whose husband caught the baby, with only me in the room with them at the hospital. The other three were having their second child. Women often think their next labor will be like their first one, but each labor is different! I have had a few near catches. One was a planned homebirth, my first one in fact, and the mom was having her first baby. He came quickly, just after the midwife walked in the door.

I would be remiss if I did not share a planned catch. I had a midwife standing by my side when I was invited to catch my fourth grandchild, my oldest daughter's third child. The adrenaline fear feeling was completely replaced with peace and joy as her head emerged into my hands. It was the best catch of all, since my heart was bursting, but I was not feeling the "Oh no!"

• • • • • •

Teresa Howard, wife to Dallas, mother to three grown children, and doting nana to four grandchildren, has been a labor doula and educator for more than 20 years, attending more than 600 births! She is a certified labor doula and lactation educator with CAPPA, a certified instructor and trainer with BOLD®TM instructor with Dancing for Birth®TM and a retired La Leche League leader. Teresa owns Labor of Love Doula and Childbirth Services, Inc., a group of doulas and educators who serve the metro area of Atlanta. She loves her career and really feels being a birth professional has been her calling.

Teresa Howard

Photo by Julie Moon.
Used with permission.

Chapter 7

Cesarean Birth and the Role of the Birth Doula

Tara Campbell, CD (DONA), BDT (DONA), LCCE

What is it like in the operating room? If you have never been inside (being a patient does not count), then it can be a bit overwhelming. It's bright, cold, and small. I hope you like blue and stainless steel because the décor is a bit drab compared to a typical L&D room.

The anesthesiologist is the boss of the room. He or she will stand at the head of the O.R. table and run the show. With their professional mixology training, anesthesiologists can quickly manage a patient's symptoms with drugs. Nausea, pain, anxiety, etc.... they get it all under control within seconds, no exaggeration. They monitor all vitals and orchestrate the moment-to-moment update on your client's overall wellbeing. The anesthesiologist is cut off (no pun intended) from the surgical area, so he or she tends to be quite chatty with the patients, giving play-by-play updates, scratching your client's nose with a gauze pad (got to love that narcotic itch), and snapping photos for the family. Most anesthesiologists love doulas in their O.R. because clients are so much more relaxed and confident. Overall, they are very friendly.

There are two obstetricians, one on each side of the patient. They will talk quietly and get into the surgical zone to deliver the baby and repair the surgical incision. Both may appear detached from other events in the O.R. as they focus to deliver this baby. They may look like two members of the bomb squad trying to defuse a bomb, with only seconds to spare, yet still remaining calm, cool, and collected. There will also be a scrub tech in the room, passing instruments and assisting the obstetricians. You won't see the nurse much, since she is rarely at the head of the table. She roams about down with the obstetricians. Her role will change once the baby is born; she will manage the contact between parents and newborn, as well as monitor the newborn's vital signs. Pediatrics is always present for a cesarean birth, usually arriving just before delivery. The pediatrician or pediatric nurse will handle the immediate newborn care and assessment, and assign Apgar scores. He or she determines all is well before leaving. If there are twins, a high-risk birth, or a baby in distress, the room will fill up quickly with other essential medical personnel. In larger teaching hospitals, attending physicians for anesthesia and obstetrics often instruct their residents, so even more people are present. Everyone wears a cap and mask, so there is no way to read facial expressions - all you see are eyes.

A Brief Primer on Anesthesia

Anesthesia can be administered through a spinal or an epidural. In a spinal, anesthesia is injected into the mother's spinal space. In an epidural, anesthesia is administered through a catheter inserted into the mother's lower back. The epidural catheter allows additional medication to be injected to extend the anesthesia for a longer period of time; that's why it's commonly used for labor. The types of epidural medications differ depending on whether they're used for labor or cesarean section. For labor, the medications are just enough to take the edge off contractions, and allow the mother some movement in her legs, while for a cesarean section the anesthesiologist uses a stronger type of medication to keep her from having any feeling below her nipple line. Because the spinal is a single injection that lasts for a finite amount of time, it's most commonly used for elective, scheduled cesareans. With both spinal and epidural, the mother is awake, usually no sedatives are given, and she should be very comfortable throughout the operation.

General anesthesia is used in less than one percent of cesarean births, usually only in emergencies, or if the mother has some medical condition that rules out the use of spinal or epidural. With general anesthesia, the mother is unconscious, and usually no support people are allowed in the operating room.

Regardless of the type of anesthesia, the patient will have a blood pressure cuff on one arm, an IV and oxygen sensor on the other arm, EKG leads on her chest, and a catheter into her bladder. An oxygen mask is usually not used if the cesarean is uncomplicated.

The Doula's Role

The doula and partner are not present for the placement or adjustment of anesthesia and the initial surgical preparations. They change into hospital scrubs and wait outside the door, or in some other designated area, until the nurse brings them in. This is a great opportunity to doula the partner, explaining to him or her what to expect in the O.R.

Why don't staff let support people in for the placement of the anesthesia? The epidural procedure is the same in L&D and the O.R., but the amount of drugs used is different and the situation can quickly change. Sometimes, the mother's blood pressure drops so low she looks panicked. The anesthesiologist expects this and quickly brings her back to a normal state, with intravenous medications and fluids. This may be scary, especially for the partner. It makes more sense for the mom to get comfortably situated before the doula and partner arrive; she is in great hands with the nurse and anesthesiologist. For some patients, for example, those who are obese or have scoliosis, anesthesia placement may take longer and the partner may start to panic, worrying something is wrong. Reassure him or her.

In the O.R., the partner will sit on a stool a few inches from mom's face. It may be difficult to tell through the surgical drapes, but the mother will be tilted slightly to her side, to keep the uterus from compressing the large blood vessels in the back, which could affect blood pressure. I usually stand just above mom's head, or between her and the partner. It's an extremely tight space with electrical and monitoring cords everywhere. Be extremely aware of every body movement. It's like playing twister or trying to step over trip wires. A blue drape will separate doula, mother, partner, and anesthesiologist from the rest of the team. Do not touch anything blue and DO NOT go below the drape - that is the surgical field!

Much happens in the first 15 minutes. There are machines beeping, suctioning sounds, smells of burning human tissue, and people chatting medical lingo. The mother and partner may be overwhelmed and anxious. The doula is the calm presence, incorporating as much from the birth plan as possible. You may be manning the iPod volume and playlist; be sure to take out the ear buds as the birth approaches.

The mother may have strange sensations and feel as if she cannot breathe if the anesthesia level creeps up too high. She might feel pressure and pulling or tugging sensations as the obstetrician maneuvers the baby out. (At my last birth, I yelled out, "Are you giving me breast implants?" That's how bad the pressure was up in my rib cage.) You'll explain what's happening, as much as the client wants to know, of course, reassuring them both that what they are seeing, smelling, and hearing is normal. Some mothers need a lot of information, talking, and distraction; others don't want as much interaction. I've had some mothers become extremely anxious if it's too quiet in the O.R., because they thought something was wrong, others get more anxious with too much chatting. Try not to keep asking her if she's okay, she is probably scared to death. Use affirmations like, "You got this," "Everything is going as planned," "You're going to meet your baby soon," etc.

In an emergency the baby is usually born in about five minutes, but it can take as long as 15 minutes in a repeat, non-emergency cesarean. Encourage the partner to announce the sex of the baby if the parents don't already know, and to go over and see the baby, while you sit with the mother. If the baby is healthy, it will be wrapped up and brought over to the partner until the surgery is over. It usually takes 45 minutes to an hour, but it will seem like forever. Encourage the partner to bring the baby up to mom's face cheek-to-cheek, while you keep snapping pictures. Continue to reassure the mother she's doing great.

Usually after the delivery, she starts to get very sleepy. This is natural and not an effect of medications. Her music and perhaps some hand or scalp massage can be helpful. Talk with the partner, reassure him or her that the surgery is proceeding well, talk about the baby, and the immediate post-op plan for supporting the mother with breastfeeding. If the baby goes to the NICU immediately after delivery, figure out who is going where. Usually I stay with the mother and encourage the partner to go with their baby, but sometimes I will go to the nursery, while the partner and mom stay together.

I usually bring my silenced cell phone to take lots of photos, but no videos unless parents and the obstetrician have granted permission specifically. I have an option for this in my contract. Some good shots are the couple before they enter the O.R., the partner waiting to be brought into the O.R., and the wall clock at the time of delivery. Of course, birth shots are always great - and even a picture of the placenta. Some parents may not want this, because of all the blood, but I suggest taking them anyway. They can always be deleted, but you cannot go back and take them later. A picture of the baby on the scale being weighed is nice, too. I usually get photographs of the baby being delivered, and I also walk over to the warmer in the O.R. to take some shots of the newborn. Ask the anesthesiologist and nurse for permission before roaming over to the newborn. They can help guide you. Be aware you will see the whole, exposed surgical incision as you walk over.

From Labor to Surgery

Moving from a labor environment, either in an urgent situation, such as fetal distress, or a non-urgent situation, like failure to progress, can be overwhelming. Use the "in your face" approach if the mother is very anxious. Be the calm person making eye contact with her, as everyone else is scrambling to get her moved. Reassure her that you will see her in the O.R. Remind her she's going to meet her baby soon.

I remember a birth where the mother was attempting a TOLAC (trial of labor after cesarean). She made it to about 6 cm after 12 hours of Pitocin augmentation. The provider was fine with letting her continue, but she looked right at me and said, "Enough, I am done." The provider suggested an epidural. The mother yelled out, "I want a spinal, I am calling this! We are done here. Take me to the O.R.!" Just before she went into the O.R., she broke down sobbing. She looked at me and said, "I am so scared, please help me." I looked at her and firmly said, "You have two options. One is we can wheel you back in the L&D room and you can keep laboring. Or two, they roll forward through these doors, your choice." She paused for about 15 seconds; I could tell the staff was frustrated because I was holding things up. She looked at me and said, "They both scare me; I don't know what to choose." I replied,

"Choose the one that scares you the least." She abruptly sat forward on the stretcher, looked around at everyone, and said, "What the hell are you waiting for? Let's go have an awesome birth already!" We all laughed.

Many moms I work with say, "I never thought it would be me." The reality is the cesarean rate in the U.S. is about 32%, so cesareans are common. Informed consent is key. It is difficult to teach new concepts in the middle of active labor, so information on effects to mother, baby, and labor must be presented in an unbiased way at a prenatal meeting. Prenatally I ask, "In the event of a cesarean, what is most important to you?" This makes some mothers very anxious, others appreciate me including this as a possibly. Mothers are much less anxious if we have to move to the O.R. if I can simply say, "Remember we talked about this at your visit," and they can reference something familiar from our conversation.

Encourage your client to include in her birth plan that having her doula present in the O.R. is important. Have her discuss this prenatally with her obstetrician, and again with the nurse when she comes into the hospital in labor. It's a nightmare to try to address this in the middle of an urgent situation. This is often when doulas get left outside the operating room. Advance planning and discussion with the nurse is one of the most valuable things you can do.

The Scheduled Cesarean

I have much more experience with scheduled cesareans because of the type of high-risk clients with whom I usually work. We have weeks or months to put a strong plan into place. Some mothers will practice relaxation techniques daily to prepare, others will formulate a great birth plan to implement in the O.R. I have seen some unique strategies. One mother was so fussy about the lighting we had her wear sunglasses. With other mothers, I've done guided imagery or massage in the pre-op area, along with many photos leading up to the birth. I think for the doula it's easier to work with a mother having a scheduled cesarean because there is no "what if." She knows this is the mode of delivery and that's it. At the prenatal visit, doula and parent(s) can address every little detail. Typically, on the day of delivery, I meet the mother at the hospital about two hours prior to the cesarean.

Post-operative

If baby is separated from the mother, I usually stay with the mother until she moves from the post-op area to the postpartum floor. This may take several hours. I usually talk with her about what will happen next. With either spinal or epidural anesthesia, she may not be able to move her legs for three to six hours, sometimes longer. Reassure her that this is normal, and she is not paralyzed. Perhaps on her way to the postpartum floor, staff will allow her to see the baby, or perhaps we will help her start using the breast pump to get that prolactin and oxytocin going. One of my favorite little tricks if they are separated is to have mom sleep and pump with one receiving blanket. When she sees the baby, I have her swap receiving blankets with the baby, so they each have one another's scent when they are apart. I usually allow her to rest, maybe tell her about how well she did in the O.R., etc. Verbal reassurance goes a long way.

If the baby comes back to the post-op area, my stay is less, typically one hour. I focus on getting the baby skin-to-skin with the mother and helping her latch the baby on. If mom is too exhausted, I typically encourage the partner to do skin-to-skin. I am usually still snapping random photos.

Obstacles in the O.R.

Practices vary from one hospital to another and among providers. Doulas may be allowed in the O.R. for one birth and restricted at the next, even at the same hospital. This happened to me. I had attended many surgical births at a hospital where my unmedicated client needed an urgent cesarean section. The nurse looked at me and said, "You wait here, you won't fit in the O.R." At first I thought she was kidding, and then I realized she meant business. By nature I am a very confrontational person, but I am able to keep it in check professionally. (I am also a great actress.) I kindly told her, "I'm in the O.R. all the time." "Not tonight you're not. You wait here," she said. WOW, on the inside I was so close to losing it. My client was crying, "Please don't leave me." The nurse looked at her and said, "One person only! It's the doula or him" (referring to the partner). The partner was ranting and raving about having me go in. I was in shock, and everyone was looking at me. I knew there was no good reason for me to be kept out, but I did not make a big scene. I calmly internalized my anger. The most important thing was for this mother to be calm and confident, to have a good and safe birth experience, and come out feeling satisfied. I leaned into her and said, "I am sorry honey; I cannot go with you. I will be right here when you return. You are in safe hands and you can do this." I waited in the rocking chair until her return. When the anesthesiologist walked back in with them, he looked at me and said, "Where were you?" Seriously? They wouldn't let me in! He apologized to me and the family. The nurse was a floater and didn't know the policy. As frustrated as I was, the clients were happy with the overall outcome and that's my only obligation.

Plan in advance as much as possible. Remind your client you cannot speak on her behalf, even in the middle of a hectic situation when decisions must be made quickly. If she is at average risk for a cesarean, I would simply remind her to put in the birth plan and discuss with the provider in advance how important it is to her to have you there. She might even speak to the anesthesiologist once she is admitted. In the event of a planned cesarean, she needs to be sure there are no restrictions from staff. She can do this by talking with her provider in advance, as well as the nurse manager on the L&D unit. You and the partner will never be allowed in the O.R. in the unlikely event that she should have general anesthesia. If you are ever asked to leave the O.R., please do so, and don't be confrontational. This is very unusual, and will likely only happen if a medical emergency occurs. Remember your code of ethics. What's important are the mother's memory of this birth and your reputation. Bite your tongue and smile because this is not your birth.

Family-Centered Cesarean Movement

Common in the U.K. and slowly increasing in the U.S., a family-centered cesarean birth is significantly different than the standard cesarean birth. The EKG leads are placed on the mother's back or side rather than her chest, to allow better access for skin-to-skin contact and early breastfeeding, and also to feel less confining for the mother. Her IV is placed in the non-dominant hand (suggest requesting this to the nurse or whoever starts the IV). Along with the blue surgical drape, there is a clear drape placed in front of the mother, separating the surgical field. When the baby is being delivered, staff lowers the blue drape, so the parents can witness the birth. During a standard cesarean, the obstetrician often doesn't hold the baby up high enough for the mother or partner to see. Clear surgical drape use is very new and not available at all hospitals yet, so please ask about this option. The baby is delivered more slowly, to mimic the big vaginal squeeze that helps express mucus and fluid from the baby's lungs. The operating room staff tries to keep conversation to a minimum, so the room is as peaceful and quiet as possible, considering it is still a surgical procedure. Skin-to-skin contact is done in the O.R. with the partner and baby. The vitals and other routine infant care are done while the baby remains on the mother or partner's chest throughout the entire surgery. This allows the baby to have better thermoregulation and conserve energy for breastfeeding in the post-op area. Overall, the outcomes and birth satisfaction rates are excellent.

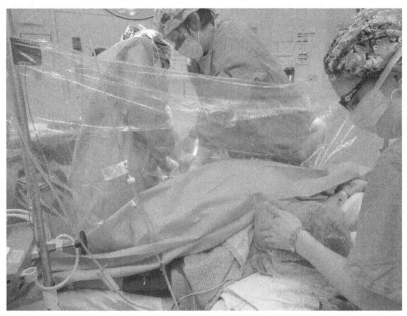

Doula working with mom in family-centered cesarean birth.

Used with permission.

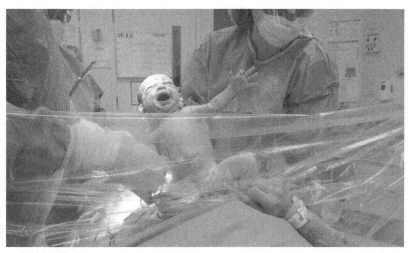

Blue drape is lowered to allow parents to see birth.

Used with permission.

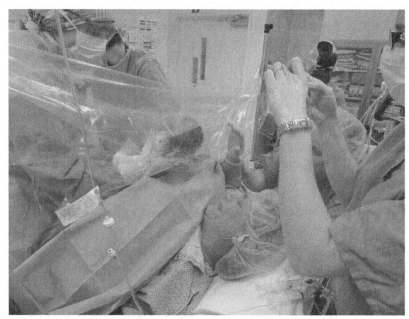

Mom sees baby right after birth through clear drape.

Used with permission.

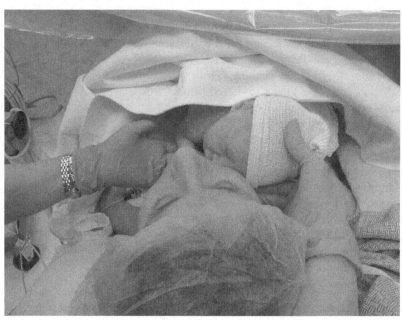

Baby is placed on mom's chest.

Used with permission.

I've had the opportunity to work with women who have experienced both types of cesarean births. The differences are amazing. The mothers are so much more satisfied with the family-centered approach. It can be a source of relief and/or empowerment to moms, particularly if the previous birth was traumatic.

Educate yourself about family-centered cesareans, so you can have meaningful discussions with medical and nursing staff. There are some YouTube videos and other online resources. Some providers have not heard of it yet. Everyone in the O.R. must be on board; it really is a team approach. What may initially appear to be a "fringe" idea can catch on and become accepted as mainstream practice, particularly as consumer demand grows. Women can put family-centered cesarean concepts in their birth plans and discuss them in advance with their obstetricians.

Your role as a doula in the O.R. is just as important as it is in an unmedicated birth. It is different, but still valuable, and in my opinion, it has been much underutilized. My best advice is ASSUME NOTHING and DO NOT JUDGE! Happy Birthing!!!

· · · · · ·

Tara Campbell, CD (DONA), BDT (DONA), LCCE, is a DONA International birth doula and birth doula trainer, and a childbirth educator. Eleven years ago, she founded Birthing Gently, a Boston and New York City-based birth doula service. Birthing Gently serves low and high-risk women, and includes a volunteer birth doula program staffed by 40 volunteers at Massachusetts General Hospital and Brigham & Women's Hospital. Tara only accepts high-risk mothers with serious medical issues who are delivering via cesarean birth at Brigham and Women's Hospital. She is currently working with the physicians, nurses, and midwives to implement family-centered cesareans.

Tara Campbell

Used with permission.

Tara's first baby was born vaginally and her other four were via cesarean because they were high risk. Two of her children have serious medical conditions - one from a birth injury, the other from congenital heart disease. She gravitated towards high-risk birth because she's definitely "been there, done that." She loves the challenge of being in a hospital environment, particularly the operating room. Tara's doula style is similar to a personal trainer's: direct, analytical, and not so touchy feely. She presents information to clients in a straightforward no-nonsense style, with humor and a twist of sarcasm.

Tara is unbiased about pain medication and believes an epidural birth can be just as satisfying as an unmedicated birth. She will support a mother no matter what her choice, and encourages women to write their birth plans in pencil, so they can edit them. For some women, relaxation comes in the form of an epidural, for others it means a warm bath, massage, and verbal affirmations, and for a few, it comes in the form of cesarean birth. As a doula, she has to put on her chameleon skins to adapt.

Her message to all new doulas is be yourself! Many new doulas worry about what clients will think of them, that they won't be taken seriously, they're too old, too young, or too inexperienced. What it boils down to at an interview is the personality match. Parents decide who they trust and want to be a part of that intimate moment in their lives. Be yourself and let the client choose, do not take it personally. She's had prospective clients turn her down. She knows she's not for everyone and is okay with that - and you should be, too. She hopes through her writing to be able to express a small fraction of what she has learned through her journey.

Chapter 8

Doula Support for Out-of-Hospital Births

Robin Gray-Reed, MSN, CNM, ARNP, IBCLC, CLD (CBI)

For centuries people have given birth at home surrounded by friends and relatives, usually women experienced in birth. Community midwives delivered the babies, and sisters and aunts helped with household tasks to allow the new family to recuperate. At the beginning of the 20th century in the United States (and paralleled around the world), a cultural shift occurred that moved the place of birth from home to hospital for most people. This was NOT an idyllic time in history. Rates of complications and maternal and infant mortality were high (both at home and in the hospital). This was before the advent of lifesaving technology and the implementation of sanitation practices to decrease infection.

Through the years, hospital births have become much safer. But recently, a notable counter-movement has arisen, growing out of a desire for greater choice and freedom in labor, as well as a reaction against medical interventions taking place in hospital births, such as routine episiotomy, restriction of movement and food intake, and instrumental or operative delivery. In some cases these interventions are certainly lifesaving for mother or baby, but they are undoubtedly over utilized. This has led to a decrease in satisfaction with the birth experience.

My Background with Homebirths

I grew up exposed to the belief that birth is, for the most part, a normal process, and barring complications, home can be a safe place to give birth. My grandmother was a nurse and midwife who attended homebirths in rural South America; she had all four of her babies at home. Many of my aunts and cousins gave birth out of the hospital as well. I remember going to my aunt's home when I was a preteen. She had just had her fifth baby (and fourth homebirth) a few hours prior, with a midwife and my mom in attendance to support her.

I have been involved with out-of-hospital births since almost the beginning of my career. The first birth I ever attended, that of my nephew when I was 19 years old, was an unmedicated hospital birth. The second birth was in a freestanding birth center, and the third was a homebirth. While I currently practice as a certified nurse-midwife in a hospital environment, I seek to promote physiologic birth where possible, much as I did outside the hospital.

There is little published research to draw from regarding doulas assisting at homebirths. Therefore, I have drawn from personal experience, as well as interviews with numerous experts from a wide array of backgrounds. Some are doulas and midwives with decades of combined birth experience; some have had homebirths themselves. Others are academics with an interest in birth, and one is the author of a novel about midwifery. Their expertise adds depth and richness to this discussion. The daughter of one even helped me name this chapter!

In this chapter I am striving to avoid the use of "she" and "her" when referring to the individual giving birth. While the majority of pregnant people identify as female, there are individuals who do not feel they fit in the gender binary and who identify as transgender, genderqueer, or something else entirely, and they become pregnant and give birth, too. My goal is to include everyone that doulas may serve in the course of their work, and I will attempt to do this as much as possible within the confines of a language and a topic that is often highly gendered. If the wording comes across as awkward, please recognize it is due to my efforts to utilize the imperfect medium of this language to acknowledge the wholeness and humanity of those who have often had this denied to them.

Homebirth: An Overview

According to 2009 data from the Centers for Disease Control and Prevention, about 0.72% of U.S. babies were born at home, an increase of 29% over the previous five years (MacDorman, Mathews, & Declerq, 2012). People choosing homebirth were more likely to be white, married, over the age of 35, and have birthed previous children. The majority of planned homebirths take place with midwives. Certified professional midwives and licensed midwives, as well as certified nurse-midwives, may be the care providers. State-by-state regulations vary widely regarding out-of-hospital birth and midwifery.

Several important differences exist between home and hospital birth. Many who choose to birth in an out-of-hospital environment (family home or a freestanding birth center) prefer this location due to a perception of greater control over the labor process; more freedom of movement, choice of clothing, and eating and drinking during labor; and a familiarity with the environment, leading to an increase in relaxation. They may see homebirth as facilitating a gentler entrance into the world for the baby and a less interventive, more personal birth experience for the birthing person.

The American Association of Birth Centers (n.d.) describes a birth center as "a place that gives you a caring, warm, and home-like environment where you are supported and respected, as well as safe and secure." In addition, the ability to labor and birth in water, if desired, is more likely to be an option outside of the hospital, though there are some hospital facilities that offer water birth.

In hospitals, continuous electronic fetal monitoring during labor is a commonplace, though not evidence-based, practice. This can make maternal movement difficult and increase the risk for potentially unnecessary medical interventions (Dekker, 2012). In homebirths midwives monitor the fetus with a handheld Doppler or (less often) a fetoscope. National recommendations for intermittent monitoring (most common at homebirths) suggest auscultating the fetal heart rate at 15- to 30-minute intervals during the first stage of labor and every 5 to 15 minutes during pushing (AWHONN, 2008).

In a hospital birth, attendants usually include the obstetrician, midwife, or family practice physician and one or two labor and delivery nurses. Personnel from the NICU, respiratory therapists, and/or a pediatrician or neonatal nurse practitioner may be called to attend the delivery if the baby has any risk factors or is showing signs of distress.

At home, there is usually a midwife plus a birth assistant (who may be a second midwife). In addition, a midwifery student may be present. All homebirth attendants providing healthcare services should be trained in basic life support and neonatal resuscitation measures. Midwives bring with them several heavy bags full of gear, including an oxygen tank, resuscitation equipment for the baby, sterile gloves, instruments, suturing supplies, and medications for mom and baby (such as oxytocin and Methergine for hemorrhage and vitamin K to prevent bleeding in the newborn).

Difference Between a Doula and a Midwife

I have had people ask me, "If I am hiring a midwife, why would I need a doula?" As a midwife who worked as a doula for many years, it is important to clarify the distinctions between the role of the midwife and the doula.

Midwives and doulas both generally choose birth work because they love being "with women" (indeed, that is the meaning of the word "midwife"). They are both skilled in providing comfort measures in labor and promoting relaxation. However, in the event of a medical concern or an emergency, the midwife's priority must shift to focusing on keeping everyone safe and healthy.

Emi Yamasaki McLaughlin, a licensed midwife in Seattle, states:

> "As a midwife who does homebirths, I tell my clients that I do emotional and physical support like a doula, but that my first priority is their clinical care. So having a doula means that they have one person whose sole job is focusing on emotional and physical support." (personal communication, May 24, 2014)

Kelly McKittrick, a Seattle-based certified nurse-midwife, agrees. "As the midwife, I'm in charge of EVERYTHING. I really see the doula as part of my team at a homebirth." (personal communication, May 24, 2014) She emphasizes that the doula "needs to be comfortable talking with the provider, and everyone needs to be on the same page."

Caring for the Person in Labor

In many regards, serving as a doula in an out-of-hospital setting is the same as in a hospital. The doula has a specific role at any birth, regardless of location, and this is distinct from that of the care provider(s). The doula provides comfort measures, position changes, and relaxation techniques. Doulas will also find themselves offering sips of water, providing counter pressure during contractions, and rubbing aching feet. Labor is labor, and the individual in labor needs support, encouragement, and reassurance, regardless of the place of birth.

In contrast to hospital birth, where medication is available for pain relief, homebirths generally do not have that option (at least in the United States; other places, such as the U.K., sometimes offer access to nitrous oxide in out-of-hospital settings). Doulas at homebirths will need to be prepared to provide continuous support and comfort measures to help with coping during the process of labor. "A doula in an out-of-hospital setting likely has to do less advocating for the family, as medical interventions will already be at a minimum, so focus turns toward continual support of the whole family," states Olivia Corrado, a doula, registered nurse, and student nurse-midwife in Spokane, Washington, who has attended out-of-hospital births. "Being really present with mom's needs, clear with communication and coaching, as pain meds are also not likely to be in use, and helping with the postpartum stage (breastfeeding support, getting mom some food, and guiding the transition into rest) is also vital."

Susan Harper, an anthropologist with a special interest in women's studies, ritual, and activism, believes that:

> "Doulas are really key to providing a sense of safe space, even sacredness, in homebirths. They help remind birthing parents that they are not just there to bring a new life into the world, but are themselves sacred and supported." (personal communication, May 26, 2014)

Similarly, Meg Elison, author of the novel, *The Book of the Unnamed Midwife*, believes that doulas are charged with multiple important tasks:

> "A doula's role in a homebirth is equal parts spiritual and practical. She must live in two realities at once, one where she watches real events of monumental importance and one where she must keep her eyes on all possibilities." (personal communication, June 4, 2014)

Seattle-based nurse-midwife Laura MacPherson had doula support at both of her births. Her first doula at her hospital birth before she became a midwife was "like a tour guide in a foreign land" (personal communication, May 26, 2014). According to Laura, doulas for hospital births have to be "knowledgeable about the space as well as about labor," whereas at home, "it seems that the couple is the expert on the space and the doula can be an extra pair of hands." She considered her second doula at her homebirth to be "a caretaker of the space," who "made herself at home and took care of things, like making plates of appropriate nourishment magically appear when needed."

Caring for the Partner

"I think the role of a doula attending a homebirth is to guide a sense of calm as families transition into labor," recommends Olivia Corrado. "They can ease the partner into their support role, showing them good language and pressure points early on, so they feel more confident as labor gets harder."

Virginia Bobro, a doula, lactation consultant, and childbirth educator in Santa Barbara, California, agrees, "Support of the dad or partner can be at the top of lists of doula's tasks, as often he or she feels like they should take a more active role at a homebirth." (personal communication, May 24, 2014) Possibly having limited birth experience, partners may feel out of their element seeing their loved one in pain and working so hard, and doulas can help to support them in providing comfort measures.

Caring for Midwives

Providing practical support for the entire birth team is a great benefit to having a doula at a homebirth. Several midwives I spoke with encourage doulas to come to a prenatal appointment to meet the midwife and develop rapport. This is also an excellent time to cover expectations for labor and answer any questions.

During labor, doulas can provide practical support, which frees midwives up to nap, run to the bathroom, or catch up on charting if birth is not imminent. Midwives are responsible for the clinical wellbeing of the family, and with a doula present to attend to other tasks, the load is eased and the midwife can better focus on the big picture.

Logistics of Birth Preparation and Cleanup

Obviously, the goal at any birth is the wellbeing of the person in labor and of the baby being born. This is as true at home as in any other setting. What is different is that at home, the family has more control over where to give birth (I've seen babies born on the kitchen floor, in the nursery, in the bedroom, in the living room, and in the bathroom!) and what the environment looks and feels like. Doulas may find themselves doing a lot more logistical work in a homebirth setting, as there are more variables to deal with, as in the following statement from a birth doula:

> "In general, be prepared for more housekeeping jobs than with a hospital birth. But don't be afraid to get in there and do hands on support and offer ideas. The client has hired you *and* a midwife for a reason. The client wants all of you there. Be there. Do your doula thing." (Rean Cross, personal communication, May 24, 2014)

A doula's job is to provide the physical and emotional support people need during labor, and sometimes this support involves somewhat mundane tasks that are nonetheless vital to the process. Doulas might need to help with laundry after the birth, getting the house in order so the new family can settle in with their baby. Birth can be a messy process, and it is up to those providing care to the family to leave the home clean and comfortable.

Sarah Osborne, a birth doula in Tacoma, Washington, has a checklist for homebirth clients of things to help her prepare for the birth. The list includes a tour of the home, ensuring she knows how to work the washer and dryer, and locations of key supplies (towels, washcloths, bowls, tea, etc.). She also brings additional supplies (a birth ball, kneeling pad, flexible straws, and a handheld mirror, among other tools) that she normally wouldn't bring to a hospital birth. During one of her prenatal home visits, Rean Cross asks her clients permission to "just poke around in their kitchen" and suggests stocking up on snacks and caffeinated drinks for the birth team.

For families choosing a water birth, doulas will often be placed in charge of filling the pool or ensuring the water remains at a comfortable temperature, and may help to empty the pool after the birth (though, more often than not, I have seen partners take on this task). If this is an expectation for the doula, it is helpful to see the tub before the birth and know where the hot water will come from and where and how the tub will be drained.

Keeping everyone fed and hydrated is an important job. The role of the doula can involve baking "labor cake" at 2:00 in the morning during early labor, prepping snacks or coffee for the family or the midwives to keep their strength up, and offering cups of cold coconut water, warm tea, or electrolyte drinks at regular intervals. Alternately, the doula may have to run to fetch a bowl from the kitchen if the mother is nauseated!

Every family has different preferences for their birth, so it is important to find out what they would like the doula to do for them. Some people want to labor in relative silence; others create a "labor playlist" and might want the doula to ensure that the music keeps playing. Some families want the special moments of their birth documented with photographs or video; others strongly prefer not to have pictures taken. If the doula will be in charge of photographing the process of labor, and no one else (i.e., a birth photographer) has been hired for this purpose, it is important to be clear ahead of time that the support role of the doula supersedes the taking of pictures.

Sibling Doulas

Some doulas offer services specifically targeted toward older siblings. Many families do not live close to relatives who can arrange to watch their other children during labor. Hiring a "sibling doula" is different than having a nanny or babysitter. Sibling doulas are experienced with birth. They typically meet with the children once or twice before labor to get to know them, and often bring books or videos on birth and sibling adjustment to help prepare them for what they might see and hear. Depending on the age and emotional readiness of the child or children, the plan might be for them to be present for the actual birth, in which case it is important for them to know what to expect. Having a doula at the birth specifically for the children, who can feed them or take them to the park or even just to another room if things get too intense for them, is important. I have been at several homebirths where siblings were in the room as their new baby brother or sister entered the world, and their reactions have ranged from straightforward questions ("Is the baby coming out of mommy's vagina SOON?!?") to eager faces peering over the top of the birth pool to grumpy tantrums related to all of the upheaval in their normal routines. Sibling support can definitely be part of any doula's role at a homebirth, but if the children are to be at home during labor, they would ideally have an adult assigned to care for them who is not a part of the birth team.

Support During Early and Long Labor

Among the midwives and doulas I interviewed for this project, there was unanimous agreement that doulas provide invaluable support to the family during early labor, at which point the midwife generally is not yet present. Midwives may stop by early on to take vital signs and check in with the family, but it is important that the midwife be rested and sharp for the birth and afterwards, so they generally do not stay with the family until active labor has begun. Rean Cross, a doula in Toronto, Ontario, adds that where she lives doulas generally arrive several hours before the midwives do. "The midwife may ask to speak with you for an opinion on how the client is doing." (personal communication, May 25, 2014)

> "I often emphasize that a client may need support early in labor, so they will call their doula," says Emi Yamasaki McLaughlin. "The midwife, on the other hand, usually doesn't come until the client is in active labor, so they may have already been laboring with the doula for a number of hours. We do it that way so that the midwife can be as fresh as possible at the time of birth." (personal communication, May 24, 2014)

Virginia Bobro agrees, "Early labor support is the real gift of a doula in a homebirth!" (personal communication, May 24, 2014)

"Midwives aren't going to be there in early labor," states nurse-midwife Kelly McKittrick. If the parents and midwife were attempting to determine whether it is time for the midwife to come to their home yet, Kelly would often ask to speak to the doula and have a conversation about what she thought. "I feel like the role of the doula is to help in early labor and give me a sense of when I need to come." (personal communication, May 24, 2014) Clearly, the decision about the midwife's arrival would be made taking all information into account, but doulas (having more experience than many partners or spouses with seeing people in labor) can serve as non-clinical "eyes and ears" in the family's home.

During longer labors, doula support can allow the midwife to get much-needed rest, so she or he can be sharp when midwifery expertise is most crucial. The first priority of the midwife will always be clinical care of the birthing person and the baby, and especially in longer labors, doulas can provide a beneficial service for both the client and the midwife, allowing the midwife to concentrate on clinical matters and helping to ensure the safety of the couplet in labor.

Postpartum Support

One beneficial aspect of having a doula at a homebirth is help in the early days after delivery. After a hospital delivery, the staff is available to help for the first day or two. At home, once the midwife feels that everyone is healthy and stable, the family is typically tucked into bed to enjoy their baby and the care team goes home. Midwives usually do home visits in the first few days postpartum to ensure the health and wellbeing of the new family. It can be wonderful in these early days to have support from the doula. Whether the couplet is having some difficulty with breastfeeding or the parents want to go over the step-by-step events of their birth with someone who was there, the doula can fill this role. (Clearly, if there are any health-related concerns or questions, these should be addressed by the appropriate care provider.) Doulas can continue to provide logistical support in the form of laundry, food preparation, and light housekeeping. Some postpartum doulas will stay overnight with families to assist with baby care and help parents get more sleep. The specifics of what support the family feels they might prefer should be discussed during prenatal meetings with the doula to ensure the services offered are a good fit for the family's needs.

Jessica Barton, a doula and lactation consultant in Goleta, California, believes doulas can provide important support for breastfeeding, both prenatally in the form of education and providing realistic expectations, as well as helping out with the initial latch and providing referrals to community resources if any long-term lactation issues arise. "As before and during the birth, the doula's role in supporting breastfeeding is to provide information and encouragement," Jessica states. (personal communication, May 26, 2014) "New parents may need help navigating their breastfeeding experience and their doula can be instrumental in guiding them, so they understand what is happening and ask all their questions." Referrals to lactation consultants, breastfeeding support groups, or the appropriate care provider (midwife or OB for suspected thrush or mastitis; pediatrician for weight-gain issues in the infant) may be necessary when issues arise that are outside the doula's scope of practice.

Scope of Practice Issues

For me personally, becoming a doula was the first step of a journey that has taken me to every birth-related course and workshop I could find, ultimately becoming a childbirth educator, birth assistant, and lactation consultant before starting nursing school and finally becoming a certified nurse-midwife. Having attended birth in various roles (doula, birth assistant, student midwife, and CNM) has taught me the supreme importance of knowing the boundaries for whatever role one currently plays and not overstepping these, even (or perhaps especially) for the sake of learning new skills for a role one aspires to someday achieve.

Early on, I remember glossing over the "scope of practice" discussion in my doula training. I wanted to get to "the good stuff" - attending births! I would learn, sometimes the hard way, that being clear about what I was and was not allowed to do as a doula served everyone's best interests. There were times when I overstepped those lines, and thankfully

I had mentors and care providers who were not afraid to pull me aside and call me on it. I remember one birth at home where I was serving as the couple's doula (I had also taught their childbirth education classes) and I began coaching her pushing. The midwife said, gently but firmly, that she would be giving guidance as it was needed, and I stepped back, embarrassed at the time, but now very grateful for the clear boundaries.

Virginia Bobro points out how important it is to be clear on one's role at a birth:

> "It can be a slippery slope for doulas to slide into 'midwife assistant' at a homebirth (for example, 'here, hold the doppler'). Doulas at a homebirth must be clear on their scope of practice - to provide emotional and practical support to parents." (personal communication, May 24, 2014)

Certified professional midwife and doula Barbara Herrera emphasizes this point:

> "Scope of practice is vital, especially for a doula who does want to be a midwife one day. It can be tempting as all get out to help the midwife (with just this, no, this, too... and this, too)." (personal communication, May 24, 2014)

In an online publication for DONA-trained doulas considering offering support at homebirths, Mattox and Lane (n.d.) encourage giving considerable thought to a number of legal and logistical issues that could arise in an out-of-hospital setting. For instance, it is important to be aware of legislation about homebirth in the doula's home state, as laws pertaining to midwifery and out-of-hospital birth vary widely in the United States. The doula should consider potential implications (including the possibility of civil or criminal charges) should a complication arise during a homebirth. The doula needs to be clear to stay within a well-defined scope of practice and refrain from giving medical advice or performing any clinical tasks or procedures (such as vaginal exams, blood pressure checks, or listening to fetal heart tones during labor). According to the DONA International document on Standards of Practice for birth doulas (2008), "The doula accompanies the woman in labor, provides emotional and physical support, suggests comfort measures, and provides support and suggestions for the partner." Clinical care - including the provision of medical advice - is strictly outside the doula's scope. In a homebirth setting, especially in the case where the midwife or care provider has not yet arrived (i.e., if labor is still early), it is vital that the doula be a part of the conversation about options, but not make decisions for the parents or the care provider.

It is outside the scope of this chapter to fully address the role of secondary trauma in birth work, but it bears a brief mention here. Incidental or repeated exposure to stressful or traumatic experiences (witnessing clients receiving less than compassionate treatment by care providers, experiencing a bad outcome, to name just a couple of examples) can cause behavioral changes that in doulas could push them toward avoidance of certain experiences. For instance, I have known of more than one doula who, after several stressful hospital birth experiences, chose to only serve couples desiring out-of-hospital births. The problem with this is that by avoiding the trauma, it does not find resolution, and it may be re-triggered if a similar event occurs (such as in the case of a homebirth client needing a hospital transfer). I would urge anyone who has experienced stress as a birth worker to explore it with a compassionate counselor or to debrief (respecting client anonymity, of course) with other birth workers. This work cannot be done in isolation.

If Complications Arise: Transfers fromHome to Hospital

Even in the best of circumstances, not all intended out-of-hospital births are able to occur without medical intervention. It is important for the doula who is serving at home or birth center births to know what their role would be during and after a transport to the hospital for further intervention, be it Pitocin and an epidural for stalled labor or an emergency cesarean section for fetal distress.

Every situation is different. For a transfer before the birth, the doula can be the element of continuity between home and hospital. Midwife Kelly McKittrick goes to the hospital to settle in the mom, then has the doula stay and be their support through the remainder of labor. In the case of a transfer for the baby after birth, a decision has to be made as to who will go with the baby to hospital and who will remain with the mom at home. Typically, partner and baby go to the hospital (sometimes with the birth assistant or second midwife, if present) and doula and midwife stay home with the mom, in which case, while still in a non-medical role, it is valuable to the midwife to have a second person who can help out at home.

> "[The doula] is not in charge, but she can be my eyes and ears while I'm in the other room. Maybe I'm packing up my gear at a homebirth, so I'm not leaving a huge mess in the house. She's the continuity for the mom. It's nice for her to have that presence." (Kelly, McKittrick, personal communication, May 24, 2014)

In the event of a transfer to the hospital, it is vital that the doula provide a sense of presence and grounding to the family in the midst of uncertainty. Home is as much a state of mind and body as it is a physical location. Helping families stay mindful and focused on the birth can mitigate the disruption caused by the change in birthplace.

On a similar note, it is important for the doula to know what to do if complications arise or baby starts coming before the midwife arrives at the home. Doula Sarah Osborne makes sure she has the family's address handy in case of an emergency where she might need to call 911 and direct emergency personnel to the home. Sometimes, babies come precipitously with no warning, and in this case, it would be appropriate to call for help and follow the instructions given by appropriate authorities, as well as to notify the midwife, so they will come quickly.

Unassisted Childbirth

I would like to discuss a controversial topic in homebirth - people intentionally choosing to birth at home without the assistance of a healthcare provider. These are not situations where the baby is simply coming too fast for the midwife to get there or the family to get to the hospital. People who choose unassisted childbirth (or UC, as it is often called) do so for any number of reasons. For some, religious or philosophical beliefs about birth motivate them to deliver alone. Laura Shanley, one of the most vocal advocates of unassisted birth, states, "birth is only dangerous and painful for those who believe it is" (2014). Others are reacting against previous negative experiences (Dannaway & Dietz, 2013). Doula Amy Wright Glenn (2014) explains that many who choose unassisted birth do so "as a result of feeling powerless and mistreated during a previous birth experience." These families, she argues, "simply have lost faith in the medical models available to them."

DONA International, the largest doula-certifying agency in the world, released a position statement (2010) on doulas attending planned unassisted births. In it, they reiterate the role and scope of the doula and urge them to consider whether attending an unassisted birth as a support person would place them in a situation where they could be expected to perform tasks that fall outside their scope, or where they could be exposed to legal action (from the family or an outside source, such as a medical provider or law enforcement personnel) in the case of an unfortunate outcome.

Barbara Herrera is a southern California-based certified professional midwife and doula who was once a supporter of unassisted birth. She delivered one of her daughters at home with friends serving as doulas, but without a healthcare provider present. The birth was complicated by a shoulder dystocia, but luckily the baby was okay. She also used to teach expectant families planning unassisted births about how to prepare for emergencies. She had a complete change of heart about UC following the deaths of several babies whose families she knew, and wrote about it on her blog (Herrera, 2012). She emphasizes, "The doula will have a very difficult time explaining their role as NOT midwifery [at an unassisted birth] if it ever went to court." (personal communication, May 25, 2014)

In theory (though, after significant searching, I was unable to find any cases where this has occurred), if something happened to mom or baby at an unassisted birth and the doula was the person present who was most knowledgeable about birth, even if the doula stayed within their scope of practice, they could be charged with practicing medicine or midwifery without a license. Ultimately, it is crucial that each doula be clear with families what they will and will not do, what their support entails, and what situations (with their associated liability) they are willing to take on.

Supporting All Families

Focusing on inclusion for the vast diversity of family configurations is one of the gifts of being a doula. We are invited into people's homes and lives for one of the most intense experiences imaginable. They entrust us with welcoming their new babies and holding space for the unfolding of their stories. People having babies are as diverse as any other group of folks - some are single, others are partnered. All ages across the span of reproductive life are represented, as are a wide variety of languages, sexualities, gender identities, ethnic and cultural backgrounds, and belief systems. Though certain groups are over-represented in homebirth families, doulas need to be knowledgeable about the special needs of the different populations they will serve throughout their careers.

Of special note is service to lesbian, gay, bisexual, transgender, and queer (LGBTQ) families. Some of these families choose to birth outside of the hospital system due to a desire to choose their birth team in advance and have more control over the people present at their birth. Many queer folks have had negative experiences with the healthcare system throughout their lives, having to explain their identities and their bodies to healthcare providers who might be homophobic or transphobic or just lacking in knowledge of how to meet the needs of this population. Simon Adriane Ellis, a queer and genderqueer certified nurse-midwife whose Seattle practice is focused on reproductive health for people of all gender identities, believes that:

> "Supporting queer families should come easy to doulas - we are, after all, highly skilled in adaptability, compassion, and centering the specific needs of the specific person or family before us. We can roll with the most amazing of punches. So having a birthing family where both parents are called mom, or where the birthing parent is called dad, shouldn't be a big deal for us. At the same time, we can't trivialize the challenges these families face, and we have an added responsibility to help families navigate these challenges with as little trauma as possible." (personal communication, May 31, 2014)

He recommends that doulas familiarize themselves with the challenges that institutionalized homophobia and transphobia impose on LGBTQ families, in addition to understanding other intersecting forms of oppression and injustice, such as institutionalized racism.

Conclusion

Doulas are a valuable part of the team at homebirths. They can promote comfort and relaxation during labor, provide logistical and practical support in the early days postpartum, and help ease the transition into parenthood. This chapter discussed some of the differences in a doula's role in an out-of-hospital birth as compared to a hospital birth. It highlighted ways that a doula can support people in labor, their partners and children, and midwives and other members of the birth team. As non-medical providers of physical and emotional support, doulas have a lot to offer at homebirths. And the reward for their labor is evident on the satisfied faces of the families they serve.

References

American Association of Birth Centers. (n.d.). *What is a birth center?* Retrieved from http://www.birthcenters.org/for-parents/what-is-a-birth-center

AWHONN. (2008). *Fetal heart monitoring.* Retrieved from https://www.awhonn.org/awhonn/content.do?name=07_PressRoom/07_PositionStatements.htm

Dannaway, J. & Dietz, H.P. (2013, April 6). Unassisted childbirth: Why mothers are leaving the system. *Journal of Medical Ethics.* DOI 10.1136/medethics-2012-101150.

Dekker, R. (2012). *Evidence-based fetal monitoring.* Retrieved from http://evidencebasedbirth.com/evidence-based-fetal-monitoring/

DONA International. (2008). *Standards of practice - Birth doula.* Retrieved from http://www.dona.org/PDF/Standards%20of%20Practice_Birth.pdf

DONA International. (2010). Statement on unassisted births attended by doulas. Retrieved from http://www.dona.org/PDF/Statement_Unassisted%20Birth_0410.pdf

Glenn, A.W. (2014). *A canary in the coal mine: The growing popularity of unassisted childbirth.* Retrieved from http://www.philly.com/philly/blogs/birth-breath-death/A-canary-in-the-coal-mine-the-growing-popularity-of-unassisted-childbirth-.html

Herrera, B. (2012). *Shifting from pro-UC to anti-UC.* Retrieved from http://navelgazingmidwife.squarespace.com/navelgazing-midwife-blog/2012/7/25/shifting-from-pro-uc-to-anti-uc.html

MacDorman, M.F., Mathews, T.J., & Declercq, E. (2012). *Home births in the United States, 1990–2009.* NCHS data brief, no 84. Hyattsville, MD: National Center for Health Statistics. Accessed from http://www.cdc.gov/nchs/data/databriefs/db84.htm

Mattox, U., & Lane, B. (n.d.). *A guide for doulas attending planned homebirths*. Retrieved from http://www.dona.org/pdfs/PracticeTopics/A_Guide_for_Doulas_Attending_ Planned_ Homebirths_13.pdf

Shanley, L. (2014). *Unassisted childbirth*. Retrieved from http://www.unassistedchildbirth. com/

· · · · · ·

Robin Gray-Reed has been passionate about promoting women's health and supporting growing families for more than a decade. She has worked as a doula, childbirth educator, birth photographer, international board certified lactation consultant, registered nurse, sexual assault nurse examiner, and certified nurse-midwife. Areas of special interest include working with LGBT individuals and families, helping facilitate breastfeeding in special circumstances, promoting mindfulness-based and trauma-informed approaches to care, and supporting survivors of trauma. She lives in the Puget Sound in gorgeous Washington State with her two cats.

Robin Gray-Reed

Used with permission.

Chapter 9

The Difference Between Homebirth and Hospital Birth for the Doula

Kim Bradlee, MW, HBCE, LLLL

In the U.S. the majority of births occur in hospitals, about 5% occur in birth centers, and only about 1% occurs in homes. As such, it's a rare opportunity for a doula to be asked to attend a homebirth. This can be an exciting and sometimes challenging experience. Most likely, there will be many differences from the standard hospital birth you are used to attending. You will still be using your doula knowledge and skills, but it's important to be open to any of these differences that might make you initially uncomfortable about your role. You'll be happy to know there will also be many similarities - you'll be welcomed as a part of the birth team and you can look forward to a great experience.

To begin with one of the differences, there is a wider range of practitioner possibilities for a homebirth. Most commonly, the practitioner will be a Licensed Midwife (LM), Certified Professional Midwife (CPM), or a Direct Entry Midwife (DEM). The practitioner can also be a Certified Nurse-midwife (CNM), Chiropractor (DC), Nurse Practitioner (APRN), Physician's Assistant (PA), or Naturopath (ND).

All of these "midwives" can have various philosophies about what is acceptable at home. Generally, the belief is that birth is normal and natural for a healthy mom and baby, and there should be no interference as long as mom and baby are doing well. This goes along with a woman's trust in her body to give birth naturally and is often why a woman chooses to have a homebirth in the first place. As the doula, you'll need to find a way to be open and supportive, and look at this as a learning experience, so you can take any new information you learn and apply it to future births.

Is a Doula Really Needed at a Homebirth?

Even though the midwife and her team will most likely be in attendance for a significant amount of time, it can be quite challenging for them to be in the role of providing support, in addition to taking care of the other tasks they need to make sure are completed. Therefore, it can be a big advantage to everyone to have a doula join the team. When you have been hired to attend a homebirth, you can expect to be providing emotional and physical support to the laboring woman. Jennie Cudmore encourages women who are planning a homebirth to hire a doula:

> "My second birth was a home birth. It was amazing, and my doula was the most important part. My back pain was incredible, and she massaged me through my whole labor. Having three women to support me during my labor and reassure me was absolutely amazing - a very different experience from my first birth."

A doula might also be hired to support the child/children who will be in the home while mom is laboring and birthing. You may need to answer questions, keep the child/children busy, and by staying calm, you will provide reassurance that everything is okay. The child/children may be present at the birth, or not, so you will need to be flexible about your expectations of seeing the actual birth. By being there for the child/children in whatever capacity they needed, you are helping the mom be able to focus on herself and her baby.

Birth Preparation

One common feature of a homebirth practice is that the midwife is able to spend more time with the woman prenatally and will be the attendant at her birth in most cases. This usually helps the woman feel a high level of comfort with her midwife and lets her discuss her thoughts about the upcoming birth in depth. They can then come up with a birth plan that's appropriate. Often, helping with the birth plan is something a doula expects to do with her client. You might not have to spend much time answering questions about what to expect during labor and birth or helping her find ways to work through any fears, but you should cover these things in case you have additional suggestions the midwife hasn't given. Remember, you were hired because the extra support is wanted, so don't be afraid to contribute and share your knowledge.

An additional feature of homebirth is that you will most likely be asked to attend a prenatal home visit to meet the midwife and anyone else that will be present at the birth. At the visit, you should go over the probable roles of everyone planning to attend. As homebirth midwife Tammy Wills says, "Doulas are great at homebirths, as long as they understand their role." That's why it's important to meet with everyone and discuss what's expected. This allows you to feel you are a part of the team, and you'll have a better idea of where you'll fit in, how you can all work together, and what to expect before labor starts.

During Labor

Depending on the circumstances, you may be asked to be with the woman in early labor before the midwife and the rest of the team arrive. If this happens, it's a nice opportunity to make a connection with your client and help you feel comfortable in the new setting. Since there is no limit to the number of attendants, there may be others in and out throughout labor. Make sure to include them if that's what your client would like.

Another possibility is that you will not be called until after the midwife has arrived, since the woman is comfortable at home and doesn't need to decide when to change locations. Either way, you'll be doing the same things to provide emotional and physical support at home as you would be doing in any other location. Working with a team can be an advantage, as it makes it possible to take time for yourself when necessary.

The usual level of advocating for your client during labor and birth should not be necessary, but the differing philosophies of homebirth might include ideas that you are unfamiliar with and could make you feel uneasy. Typically, a homebirth midwife does not use active management of labor, so some differences you might see are as follows:

- No vaginal exams.

- Acceptance of many different patterns of contractions.

- Encouragement for the woman to follow her body's lead in pushing.

- No time constraints as long as mom and baby are doing well, even during the pushing stage.

- Encouragement for the woman to be in any room or position in which she feels comfortable.

- No view of the baby during descent due to the woman's position.

- A totally hands-off approach by the midwife when the baby is emerging.

- Encouragement for the woman to catch her own baby or to have her partner or someone else catch the baby.

Because of these or other differences, some doulas may feel uncomfortable. This is the time to follow the caregiver's lead, but don't be afraid to talk to the midwife or someone else on her team. It is okay to get more information when appropriate, so you feel comfortable in supporting your client. As homebirth midwife Danielle Kilroy says:

"For a doula at a home birth, there is no stupid question, especially if this is a new experience for the doula. If you don't know, ask away! And after the baby comes, try to make a time to ask any questions of the midwife, so you can better support the mom at the next birth."

The remote possibility of an emergency can be scarier for a doula at a homebirth, since it's happening outside of a medical atmosphere. Typically, once the midwife is there for active labor, she usually remains present for the duration. This makes it easy for you to get reassurance that everything is going well. If there is an emergency, it's important to stay calm and do whatever is asked of you.

After the Birth

A homebirth tends to be very relaxed once the baby has been born. There is much less of a time limit on what needs to happen next. It's all on mom and baby's time. This could mean that you are free to leave soon after the birth, even if much else hasn't happened yet. If you choose to stay, you can help with cleanup, nursing, and getting the family settled in for a rest.

The postpartum period is a wonderful time for the mom to have access to as much support as is needed. This is where you might feel most comfortable, since there shouldn't be any differences in what you do during this time.

Conclusion

What it comes down to is that, same as always, you are there to do what you can to make sure the birth is a positive experience for your client and her family. Then you will have had a positive experience, also.

• • • • • •

Kim Bradlee has been attending homebirths as a midwife for more than 20 years. She is also a hypnotist, childbirth educator, breastfeeding counselor, and mother of three. When she is not working, she enjoys spending

Kim Bradlee (top left) and family

Used with permission.

time with family, especially her 95-year-old grandmother, Frances Cohen Paone. You can reach her at Alternative Birth Care.

Chapter 10

Food Is Love – Caring for the Postpartum Family One Cookie at a Time

Ann E. Tohill, CLD, CPD

Each time I meet with a family during our initial prenatal or postpartum visit, I have a standard list of questions. I ask what led them to their decision to work with a doula, prenatal care and concerns, birth plans and intentions, comfort measures, prenatal and childbirth education, views on pain management during labor, postpartum plans and concerns, breastfeeding, infant care, and some basic health history information. We typically talk from one to three hours during the first visit. Towards the end of each meeting, we begin to discuss the postpartum period, and that's when we get to chatting about the really important stuff. Cookies.

It might seem a little odd and out-of-place for a discussion focusing largely on childbirth and comfort measures, but one of the things I love most about a postpartum visit is showing up to the client's home with freshly baked cookies. The morning of a postpartum appointment, I prepare a batch of dough, bake two-dozen cookies, then roll the rest of the unbaked dough in parchment paper, twist up the ends, write the baking instructions directly on the paper, and freeze it. The families can then slice off as few or as many cookies as they want, even in the middle of the night during a marathon nursing session, and within ten minutes, they have freshly baked cookies.

It's a very simple, little thing I do that seems to go a really long way with my clients. There's just something so lovely about freshly baked cookies at 4:00 a.m., with virtually little-to-no preparation, noise, or major clean up. I always throw some rolled oats in there for the potential galactogogue effects and nutritional benefits, of course. Virtually any traditional cookie dough will work for this. I've written one of my favorites below:

Oatmeal Chocolate Chunk Cookies

2 sticks unsalted butter at room temperature

¾ cup granulated sugar

¾ cup firmly packed light brown sugar

2 large eggs at room temperature

1 tsp vanilla extract

1½ cups all purpose flour

1 tsp baking soda

¼ tsp fine sea salt

2 cups rolled oats

1½ cups semi-sweet chocolate chunks or chips

Preheat oven to 350 degrees. Line two baking sheets with parchment paper.

In a large mixing bowl, or using a stand mixer, beat together the butter, granulated sugar, and brown sugar on medium speed until smooth and creamy. Then add eggs and vanilla, and continue to mix until smooth.

In a separate bowl, combine flour, baking soda, and sea salt. Reduce mixer speed to low and slowly add the flour mixture, and continue to mix until smooth. Stir in the oats and chocolate chunks or chips until combined.

Using a rounded tablespoon, scoop and place cookie dough onto the prepared baking sheets, spacing them about 1½" apart. Bake until golden brown, about 10-12 minutes. Transfer cookies onto a wire rack to cool completely.

If you are not going to bake the entire batch at once, roll remaining uncooked dough into parchment paper and freeze immediately.

As a postpartum doula, I love preparing foods for my clients that are not only nutritious and wholesome, but also fun and delicious. I take any and all requests, and thankfully, no one has asked me to deep fry a turkey or make anything incredibly outlandish…yet. I like to make foods in large batches, so the family has a stocked refrigerator and freezer for easy meal options after I've gone home. Soups and stews always seem to be a big hit during the colder months here in Vermont, and I like to bake a batch of cheddar scallion popovers in their home while we're waiting for the soup to warm on their stove. I also create colorful salads and make my own dressing for the family, which I leave with them in a glass jar. I love cooking foods that will keep mom feeling cared for and satisfied after her labor. I've read that a woman can burn somewhere in the neighborhood of 50,000 calories during her labor. I'd say that's a pretty great excuse to eat a few (dozen) cookies!

Another client favorite is my butternut squash risotto cakes. These are great! I make them in a large batch, shaping and freezing the remaining cakes to be baked later. They make a delicious, easy dinner paired with a salad for later. They bake up effortlessly and taste fantastic any time of day or night!

Cooking for clients is even more rewarding when I involve their older children in the experience. I have come up with many family-friendly recipes that are great to make with the kids, while mom sits back and (mostly) relaxes with her newborn. We've made fresh maple yogurt, fresh paneer cheese for our masala, pizza dough from scratch for decorate-your-own-pizza night, farmer's market salads with fresh dressing, and Thai peanut noodles with loads of fresh veggies and tofu. It is so rewarding to work with the kids and teach them about fermentation, live cultures, local farms and seasonal foods, cheese making, patience (yogurt takes seven hours!), and most importantly, fun and experimentation with different foods and flavors in the kitchen.

I love to hold newborns while their families eat in peace and quiet, able to share a rare moment together at the table. Once dinner is finished, I clean up the entire kitchen and dining area, put everything away, including leftovers, and do my best to leave their home in better shape than it was when I arrived. I also stock their refrigerator and offer breastfeeding support, nursery management tips, babywearing support, infant soothing techniques, help with laundry, help with processing their birth, and anything else they may need during our visit that is within my scope of practice.

I find it's the little things - freshly baked cookies, cooking projects with older children, and clean sheets on a mother's bed - that leave her feeling cared for and pampered. Isn't that what every postpartum family deserves? Ask a mother what she would love to try, but hasn't had the time to prepare for herself. Is there a recipe on Pinterest she's been eyeing for a long time, but hasn't been brave enough to attempt? I recently had a client send me a Pinterest recipe for sea salted caramel stuffed cocoa crinkle cookies. A mouthful in every sense.

The fun part for me is baking a test batch at home, "just to make sure" it's a good recipe, before making a batch for the client. My family has certainly benefitted from my trial runs, and so have my clients! Take the time to experiment and try out new things to add to your cooking and baking repertoire. You may find this is just what you need to get yourself out of the slump of making the same old things day in and day out. And what client doesn't love ordering and receiving exactly what they're craving at the moment? Have fun with it and bon appetit!

· · · · · ·

Ann E. Tohill, CLD, CPD has been a stay-at-home mom in the Mad River Valley of Vermont since 2009. She has a BA in English and Irish Literature, and studied Latin and Ancient Greek at Muhlenberg College, Allentown, PA. While living in Vermont for 15 years, Ann has been a preschool teacher, an editor, a restaurant owner, and a vegetarian chef.

Being a doula at Mountain Mama Doula allows Ann to turn her passion for cooking, as well as birth and family care, into a rewarding and fulfilling career.

**Ann Tohill
and Marley Hannah**

Photo by Heather Kurey.
Used with permission.

Ann has the immense honor and privilege of caring for Vermont families prenatally, during their births, and during the postpartum period. She loves supporting families in welcoming their babies into the world, and then caring for them in their homes, offering postpartum support with breastfeeding, household management, babywearing and comfort techniques, and her absolute favorite, caring for the whole family with meal preparation. She lives with her husband, two children, a couple of cats, and a happy little flock of Bantam hens and roosters.

Chapter 11

Friends & Clients

Jenny Everett King, CCCE, Doula

A doula is not a friend, my website reads. *A doula is a trained professional.* Like most birth workers, I cringe when I hear reasoning like, "Oh, I don't need to hire a doula. My sister will be there," or, "I'll be in a hospital, but with a midwife, so is a doula really necessary?" As tactfully, but as adamantly as possible, I try to respond to such misconceptions. I work to reinforce the idea that doulas have a unique scope of practice - their own irreplaceable role at birth.

The fact that we find ourselves outlining these differences demonstrates the unusual nature of our jobs. Imagine a physician needing to clarify ahead of time, "I am not here to be your friend." Picture a nurse saying, "I am able to provide you with support free from the emotional ties a family member has." No other field combines such intimacy and professionalism into one role. A doula may find herself explaining effective comfort techniques one moment, the difference between natural and synthetic oxytocin the next - and the moment after that, securing her client's hair into a ponytail as she speaks calm words of reassurance and helps her to the toilet. Prenatally and postpartum, we talk with our clients not only about their medical histories, but about their relationships with parents and siblings, their deepest fears surrounding birth and parenting, and their sex lives. Our role is neither medical nor maternal, yet it can often feel like an unusual melding of the two. Doctors, midwives, and nurses need not concern themselves with negotiating this privilege, this question, this liability. No, this sort of emotionally intimate terrain is unique to doula work.

Due to the varied and uncommon nuances of our role, navigating boundaries with clients can be difficult. A professional doula will typically use a contract to clearly outline her relationship with the client, to define both expectations and services provided. Some doulas elect to keep their personal and professional lives completely separate, with no room for possible overlap. Others choose not to fret over the potential complications of a closer relationship, and befriend their clients with ease. The majority of us, however, fall somewhere in the middle. Eventually, most doulas will encounter a situation in which a signed contract does not adequately reflect her relationship with the client, either professionally or personally. Especially for those of us who are peers with women of childbearing age, it is important to explore the edges of these relationship boundaries and to reach individual conclusions regarding the types of ongoing relationships with which we are comfortable.

While most of us find that our clients - individuals with their own needs, desires, backgrounds, and personalities - cannot be placed in boxes, there are two broad categories with which we can begin to address the question of friendship and boundaries. Here are two general situations a doula can expect to encounter at least once, probably more, over the course of her career - the potential to develop a lasting friendship with a client and the opportunity to support an established friend during her birth. While in some cases with particular individuals, it might be appropriate to decline such opportunities, I have found that often, these more intimate client relationships not only lead to rich friendships, but also give us deeper insights into the nature of the work we do with all clients.

The Client Who Becomes a Friend

Becky and I liked each other immediately. Our consult included no awkward greetings, no first moments of tentative chitchat, as we felt out the meeting. Instead, our interaction felt easy and natural. We discussed, as always, her pregnancy, her plans for birth, and what I had to offer. We looked at the contract in detail. By the end of the hour, I was informally hired.

My doula partner knew in advance that she would be away leading a training the week of Becky's due date, so unlike most DeviBloom clients, Becky was exclusively mine. In addition to our regular visits, she also took prenatal yoga with me for several months, which provided us with further opportunities to talk about natural coping techniques, her anxieties surrounding birth, and her postpartum plans. Towards the beginning of her third trimester, I became pregnant myself. I waited to share the news with my clients and students until we heard our baby's heartbeat for the first time. When I told Becky, the shared experience only seemed to enhance our relationship. Clients are, understandably, always curious to learn the choices a doula makes for her own pregnancy, and Becky was no different. By the time she was full-term, we felt as if we knew each other quite well.

Her labor was fast and uncomplicated. Days past her due date, her membranes ruptured, and with the luxury of living close to the hospital, she stayed home until her contractions became intense. When she was checked in triage, she was 9 cm dilated.

The delivery was lovely - fast, straightforward, unmedicated, powerful. We were both shocked, therefore, to learn she had experienced significant tearing. It was while holding her hand, keeping her distracted, and admiring her baby during the long repair - significant enough that the nurse-midwife who attended the birth called in the hospital OB for suturing - that I first began to question myself: How had this happened?

Could I have helped to prevent it? Should I have done anything differently?

To this day, Becky says no, I was just what she needed in a doula. I am glad to hear it, and logically I know that there may be nothing I could have done. But still, I have my questions. I wonder if I fell too easily into the friend role, encouraging her as she pushed, excited

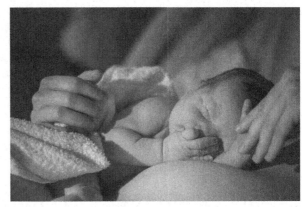

Becky's baby

Photo by Jenny Everett King.
Used with permission.

for her birth, perhaps more emotionally attached to the outcome than I typically am. I neglected to suggest she breathe her baby down. When she moved from hands and knees to squatting and began to push with impressive force, I was thrilled that she had found an effective position. But when her baby's head emerged just two pushes later, covered in her bright red blood from the tears, I suddenly remembered that encouragement is not my only job when a mom is pushing. Had I been more in my left brain, had I been more careful to see Becky as a client who hired me to support her birth in *every* way, and not just as a friend who asked me to encourage her, I wonder if that tearing could have been prevented. It was not my responsibility, of course; it is not even within my scope of practice to prevent injury or to preserve tissue integrity, but I know that for a few moments I fell too easily into the role of cheerleader.

After our first postpartum visit, when I received a beautiful thank you letter expressing her appreciation for not only my services, but for me personally, I began to realize the client-friend boundary was blurring. I was not bothered by this fact, but as I recognized that it was not typical for my doula role, I sought out the advice of other doulas. Did they befriend their clients? Did they consider friendship to be inappropriate?

The wisdom I received was simple and nearly unanimous: it is not inappropriate to become friends with a former client. However, a newly postpartum woman is not capable of forming a peer relationship with her doula. Why? Because she still needs me to be her doula, not her friend. The prospect of friendship was best left to lie dormant, to remain in waiting, as I continued to support Becky on a professional level. When she needs me less, when her role as a mother becomes firmly established, then it will be the right time to pursue a mutually supportive friendship.

As Becky adjusts to life as a new mom, our relationship continues to blossom. We chat via text and on Facebook - unlike most clients, she has friended me personally, not just liked my business page. We are in the same online babywearing group, where she praises my doula skills on a regular basis. She has expressed an interest in visiting my church, in learning more from me about not just birth, but also motherhood, attachment parenting, and homeschooling. I feel confident that as her baby grows, as we both gain distance from the professional, formal, *paid* beginnings of our connection, we will become close friends and ultimately enjoy a mutually supportive, peer-to-peer relationship. For the time being, I am content to witness and support a client as she becomes a mother in her own right - even as I admit to myself that she is one of my "favorites."

The Friend Who Becomes a Client

Perhaps an even more common opportunity is the one to support our friends when they give birth. When a woman is preparing to have a baby, deciding who among her nearest and dearest she wants present, the friend who happens to be a professional birth worker quickly becomes the obvious choice for many. Yet doulas who have attended the births of friends - usually at a greatly reduced fee, if they charge at all - often report that the nuances of such an arrangement are anything but obvious. My experience as Shannon's doula matched exactly what I have heard from others in the same situation: acting as a doula for a friend can be surprisingly emotional, complicated, and difficult to navigate. When you doula for a friend, I discovered quickly, nothing is a given. The usual boundaries do not exist - boundaries most of us have in place for good reason.

Shannon is my closest friend from nursing school. Her first child was born via emergency cesarean, diagnosed with a rare and usually fatal genetic disorder at two weeks old, and passed away at 19 months. She was open and honest about her experience with him; the months spent in the NICU and then the PICU were essentially what had brought her to the nursing profession. Three years later, she delivered a healthy baby via scheduled repeat cesarean. For her third birth, Shannon was planning a vaginal birth after two cesareans (VBA2C) in a high-risk facility. As an RN, she was keenly aware of the importance of adequate support when going to a hospital, yet hoping to avoid medical intervention. She asked me to be present as her doula and birth photographer.

Though I agreed without hesitation - my first VBAC! I quickly noticed the differences between working with a friend and with a typical client. Initially, I glossed over the standard prenatal visit. I reasoned, as Shannon did, that we could comfortably do away with such a formality. We knew each other well, we communicated effectively, and I was already knowledgeable about her past birth experiences. Prenatal visits seemed unnecessary at best, if not a complete waste of time and babysitters.

As Shannon approached her third trimester, though, questions about her care, including the true likelihood of VBAC, became more frequent. When she called upset after a routine OB appointment, I suggested we try to get together face-to-face and chat uninterrupted. We were unable to find a time that worked, however, and when we finally did get together, it was a play date for our kids at a local park. We talked coping strategies as we pushed our kids on the swings.

"Have you thought about taking any birth classes?"

"Eh, I don't feel like I need to. I mean, I know how it works."

Her potty-training son spoke up and requested a trip to the restroom. When they returned, she said, "I guess I'm most worried about what to say if they offer me an epidural. I don't want one, but I'm afraid of how much it will hurt and I think I might give in if they offer."

I started to say, "Do you have a birth plan? I can help you write one…." But before I could go further, my toddler tripped over a tree root and skinned her wrist. After several more tries for genuine conversation, each thwarted by the needs of small children, we called it a day. I rattled off an hour's worth of birth prep information, as we folded beach towels and buckled car seats, and made mental notes of the specific birth preferences she mentioned, as I handed her a bottle of sunscreen. And then our attempt at a prenatal visit was over.

As Shannon's due date approached, she encountered conflicting opinions from the various doctors within the OB practice handling her care. One recommended induction at 39 weeks, in hopes of giving her ample opportunity for a vaginal birth before the pressure for a repeat cesarean section increased. I offered her studies on VBAC inductions, but she declined to look into it further, explaining that research was creating stress. As her doula, I reminded myself, my job was to support her choices. I let go of my personal opinions and consoled myself with the knowledge that she seemed informed.

Anticipating a slow induction, Shannon suggested I stay home at first and come to the hospital once the Pitocin took effect and progressive contractions were underway. I went to bed early, my alarm set for 5:00 a.m., while Shannon and her husband checked into the hospital. When Shannon arrived at labor and delivery, however, the obstetrician on shift refused to proceed. She believed starting Pitocin would hamper Shannon's chances of delivering vaginally and ultimately recommended she return home. At midnight, Shannon called me in tears from her hospital room. She was frustrated by the mixed messages and beginning to feel labor would never happen. She was convinced she'd wind up with a third cesarean.

With lengthy prodromal labor, Shannon was in and out of the hospital, several times making the 45-minute drive to the high-risk hospital she had chosen for delivery. She and her husband spent a fortune on hotel rooms, gas, parking, and meals out, but her concerns about uterine rupture prevented her from straying too far from the hospital. With contractions seven minutes apart for hours, she asked me to meet them in the city, believing that this time, surely the doctor would agree to induce or augment her labor. We did some rebozo work at a local park, ate a leisurely lunch through which she contracted regularly, and returned to the hospital. The resident declared her 1 cm dilated, 20% effaced, with a posterior cervix. Go home. They opted for another night in a hotel room.

The next morning brought another tearful phone call. This time, finally, we were completely candid. She said, "My body already failed at this once." I spoke more forcefully than I had in the whole nine emotional months of her pregnancy. "No it didn't. Your body never had the chance to do this before." Her first labor had been heavily medicated due to ruptured membranes, resulting in a cesarean section for failure to progress, and left her with an unexpectedly sick baby who had been unable to fully participate in the birth process; her second was a scheduled surgery prior to the onset of labor. She continued to cry. Suddenly, I found myself speaking more insistently, more urgently, than I would dream of doing with a regular client: "Shannon. You are afraid. You have every reason to be afraid. Your last two experiences were not good. The last time you labored was with Connor, and he was very sick. You have never had the opportunity to do this before. I think you need to process your anxiety about that before you'll let yourself go into labor." I was in dangerous territory here, well outside my scope of practice and bordering on psychological counseling. As an afterthought, I added, "I'm not saying this as a doula. I'm talking as your friend now."

Early the next morning, she called from the hospital. Her water had broken two hours after we talked. She had been admitted at 4 cm.

I pondered all of this as I drove down to Boston. Had my words helped? And if they had, how should I feel about that, considering the fact that saying them at all took me outside my doula role? Is it a blessing or is it a curse that friends are not subject to scope of practice?

When I arrived, the nurse allowed me in, along with Shannon's mother, for a quick hello, then shooed us both away so she could rest with an epidural. I spent most of Shannon's labor in the waiting room. Her husband came out with the occasional update, told us she was dozing. It was the most time I have ever spent in an L&D waiting room - always an uncomfortable place for a doula to be, with a client down the hall laboring without her planned support. Why was I out here?

I got lunch, chatted with her mother, surfed Facebook, and watched the clock. At four o'clock in the afternoon, Shannon's husband invited us back. As we followed him to her room, he mentioned, "We can see the top of the head, finally. She's been pushing for about two hours."

I nearly stopped in the hallway; I was so surprised. I had to fight the urge to scream. I had spent hours bored in a waiting room and not only had she dilated fully, now she was *pushing?* Had been pushing for *hours?* They were inviting me back because they "thought I would like to see the birth." I was at a loss. I watched her son born, surrounded by nurses and doctors, unable to even squeeze in at her bedside. There was no leg for me to hold. I snapped a few quick photos before the thoroughly gowned nurse informed me that cameras were forbidden during the delivery itself. I stood near the foot of the bed, watched between the shoulders of medical staff as his head and then his body emerged. As he was born, I stood there wondering, *Why am I here?*

In the aftermath, Shannon was happy. She "got her VBAC," as they say. After her months of worry and wondering, I should have been ecstatic for her, and I tried to be. I did my best to let her think I was, as I took photos of her holding her baby, smiling, glowing. She was tired from some of the medication she had been given - I had no idea what, I realized - so

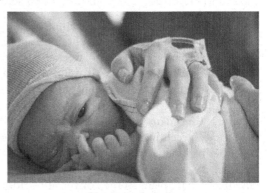

Shannon's baby

Photo by Jenny Everett King.
Used with permission.

she gave their son to her husband. An outsider would have looked upon a scene of happy young parents, a birth gone right. As an insider - or at least, so I had understood myself to be until now - I was confused. Why hadn't they invited me in? Why had she consented to so many of the interventions she hadn't wanted, without once asking me about them? Why had they even wanted a doula? Did they actually think this was my role, to hang out in waiting rooms and then come "see" a baby born? I wondered if Shannon and her husband truly understood what I do for a living, if they knew how few of my services they had utilized.

On the rare occasions a client needs space, I don't think twice about it. Waiting room while you nap? Time alone with your husband? Sure, no problem. I'll be down the hall if you need me. The desire for space or alone time has never caused me resentment or misgivings. No, I realized the issue was not with Shannon, it was with me. I had gone to visit my sister in New York, a three-hour drive from Boston, only ten days before her due date. (And then didn't sleep all weekend, lying in the guest room waiting for my phone to ring.) I had not worked with her to prepare for birth, not insisted on formal prenatal visits, not set aside the time to truly be her doula. I reasoned, albeit subconsciously, that I was working for free, therefore, the bare minimum was acceptable. I was doing her a favor, after all.

How could I have expected Shannon to take me seriously as her doula when I hadn't taken her seriously as my client?

If setting boundaries and outlining expectations are important when it comes to working with the typical client, they are ten times as important when we work with personal friends. I wish that when Shannon first broached the subject of my being there, I had suggested a consult. At the time, it felt oddly formal, almost silly. In retrospect, I believe it could have impacted both her birth and our friendship in a positive way. We both owed it to her birth to take our agreement seriously.

The question of backup is important, for both our clients and ourselves. Every doula needs a break from life on-call, certainly; every doula deserves a vacation or at least a weekend away from home. But even more than that, doulas need peace of mind when faced with the prospect of illness, or car trouble, or a family emergency. It is too easy to feel that the quality of a family's birth experience rests on our shoulders. (It doesn't, of course, but many doulas feel this way, especially in their early years of practice.) To feel this same pressure and responsibility while being on-call is neither productive nor healthy; therefore, backup is a must for our own wellbeing. When acting as a doula for a friend, it is essential to include talk of alternate plans in the conversation addressing boundaries and expectations. This may not mean that mom hires a professional doula to cover in the event that you are unable to attend, but it means that some kind of plan is in place, however subpar it feels in comparison. Perhaps another birth-knowledgeable friend can be present, or perhaps you, mom, and dad can meet together with a doula-in-training. No, it will not be the same as having her close friend by her side, but it will mean that the bases are covered.

Rebekah Labell is a Bradley childbirth educator and La Leche League leader. While she does not market herself as a doula, she attends a few births each year in order to keep her Bradley certification current. Usually these are the births of students from her class or from LLL, select individuals with whom she has developed a closer-than-usual relationship. When I asked her about the experience, Rebekah highlighted another unique issue when doulaing for a friend: the question of backup. She writes, "These women wanted ME there - and I'm not inflating my importance here. When I asked them during pregnancy...the answer for all three was 'I just want YOU there' (R. Labell, personal communication, January 11, 2014)."

However we choose to approach the prospect of attending the births of friends, it is crucial to go into the process with our eyes - and, to a certain extent, our mouths - wide open. Women preparing for birth benefit from a sensitive form of directness and candor, as well as a clear understanding of the roles their support people will take. Whether we are working for a professional client with whom we connect more than usual or with a personal connection who simply wants her birth junkie friend in the room when she has her baby, both doula and mother owe it to themselves to thoughtfully consider and discuss the nature of their relationship and the expectations on either side.

Doulas know that a mother in labor has little interest in decorum or pretense. The moments of birth have a remarkable way of stripping away social niceties and affording us the chance to see life at its most genuine. Occasionally, such rawness in birth takes families by surprise. As doulas, we have the opportunity to help mothers and their partners prepare for such moments by being candid and real ourselves in the prenatal period. Our friends, in particular, deserve to see us for who we are, what we do, and what we can offer, and they deserve to hear us explain it in advance. What better way to help the women we love most prepare for those powerful moments than to approach their pregnancies the way we hope to see them approach their births - empowered, honest, and open.

· · · · · ·

Jenny Everett King is a CAPPA certified childbirth educator and also a doula, as well as a prenatal yoga teacher, birth photographer, blogger, and homeschooling mother to four. She holds a BA in Liberal Studies in the Great Books from Saint Anselm College and has practiced and taught yoga since 2002, studying primarily in the Iyengar and Anusara methods, with a special focus on women's reproductive health.

**Jenny Everett King
and her children**

Used with permission.

Jenny's interest in pregnancy and birth has been a lifelong passion, but her journey to birth work began in earnest with her first daughter's birth in 2006. This experience helped her discover that birth has the potential to be empowering and transformative for families. Her approach to pregnancy and birth care is rooted in the idea that childbearing is not only a physical process, but an emotional journey, as well as a spiritual high point for many women. Jenny is the co-owner of DeviBloom Wellness & Birth, LLC, and can be reached at jenny@devibloom.com.

Chapter 12

Attending the Births of Friends

Amy L. Gilliland, PhD, BDT (DONA)

Courtney: "I was so excited when she became pregnant. They'd been trying for a while and she'd met me during my first pregnancy a few years ago. It seemed like we talked every few days and I was able to share what I'd learned about pregnancy and doctors. It was just assumed I would be her doula, I don't think either of us thought about bringing someone else into the picture. Our husbands got along great, too, so we had this nice couple relationship, as well as bonding over her pregnancy. As her due date approached, I was even more excited than she was! Like most of my clients, she was planning on a natural birth without medication and had chosen a supportive doctor and hospital.

Looking back on it now, I wonder whether it was our friendship that influenced her or if I didn't give her the room to choose what she wanted. I felt such a strong bond and wanted the best for her, her baby, and her husband. There wasn't any intention on my part to have her do what I wanted, but it was really hard to let go when the labor started to get tricky.

Everything started just fine, slowly, but fine. Then when we got to the hospital, she was about 5 cm and feeling a lot of pain. I encouraged her to try getting in the tub or at least the shower. At one point, she said she needed a break and went into the bathroom with her husband. She asked me to go get something out of the car. When I came back, they were prepping her for an epidural. I was kind of bewildered and annoyed, but I put on my doula hat and just went with it. The labor went okay after that, and she ended up with a vaginal birth. I held her legs and coached her, but she didn't want to look me in the eyes like she had at the beginning of the labor. The baby is two months old, and I've only seen them twice. She doesn't want to talk about the birth; she just switches the subject back to the baby. So it's between us, and I don't know what to do. As her doula I'd let it go. As her friend I want to ask her about it. Either way, at this point, she's got to lead, not me. But I miss her friendship and helping her postpartum. I know that even when we do work it out, it will never be the same."

Abby: "One of the reasons I took the doula training was to help my sisters at their births. I'd had such a great experience with my midwife that I wanted to help other people. None of my other family members would work as hard as I did to research options or choose care providers. I figured that if I had the expertise, I'd be able to help them more. Well, it was a good idea in theory, but that's not the way it turned out. I couldn't make a dent in their choices, and most of the time all I could do was hold their hand. One of my sisters ended up with a cesarean section - which was her husband's fault. He never asked a question about anything. My other sister had an epidural with a vacuum extraction. It was so painful for me to watch because I knew that they were just being impatient. I felt so helpless. Now they've both got problems, and I want to say, "I told you so," but I also feel really bad. It's just like what happens to lots of women. Only they were my sisters, and I thought I could make it better, but I couldn't."

Cassie: "It was the best labor support for me ever. I knew exactly what she wanted because I knew her so well. Her husband trusted me, and when I said they should ask more questions, they did. Everything went pretty smoothly, and we were able to make jokes. It was so relaxed, no tension. When they baby was born, I had tears coming down my face! That just does not happen for me, but I was so happy for them I couldn't help it. She's four now, and I've loved watching her grow up."

Monique: "The hardest part for me is that I know stuff about this family. When Dad was being a jerk, I had a hard time giving him some slack. I wanted to say, "Get your butt over here and get off the phone." But I couldn't because he knows me, and then I'm being judgmental and critical. If I was their hired doula, I could say, "Uh, if you could get off the phone sooner, that'd be great, because she really needs your help." I can't be my usual doula self because they'd know when I'm faking it. I'm not faking it when I'm someone's hired doula because I don't know them. It's just so much harder when you know someone. Next time a friend asks, I'll tell them I'll come *as their friend*, but they ought to hire a doula, too. I can help with labor support, but I can't doula them."

Maggie: "I miss them terribly. It was such an awful, such an unexpected, just gut wrenching thing to happen. I can't imagine it happening again that way, but I've talked to other doulas and its happened to them, too. We'd been friends for ten years, been through relationships and break ups, and then finding our husbands together. It's so hard to not have her in my life anymore. So when they got pregnant, of course, I was their doula. She'd heard so many birth stories from me, just ate them up actually, that when it was her turn, she decided on a birth center with a midwife. They did all the right things, ate the best foods, exercised - it was a stellar pregnancy. At the labor, they had candles, singing, and people praying for them - it was such a beautiful, glowing atmosphere. I worked alongside the midwife and her assistant, and the baby sounded fine the whole time.

Second stage took quite a while, which seemed odd, but we figured maybe there was a malpositioning that needed to resolve. As the baby was close, she got out of the tub to squat and moved into hands and knees for the actual birth. Immediately I knew something was wrong. They started working on him right away. I've never seen a baby look so white. The EMT's came and transported him and dad to the hospital. I followed in my car, and when I got to the hospital, the baby was dead. He'd never breathed on his own. Mom wasn't stable yet, so she had to stay at the birth center. They wouldn't let Dad leave with the baby, so we waited alone together for more than four hours.

For the next ten days, we were inseparable. Our grief bonded us, and then they stopped calling. We saw each other intermittently over the next few months, but nothing after that. When I emailed or wrote a card, I didn't hear anything. I got a holiday card and a birthday card, but nothing really warm or like, "Let's get together." They did let me know that the autopsy showed there was something wrong with the baby that wasn't her fault. It wouldn't have mattered if the baby was born in the hospital, it still would've died. It's been two years now. I heard they moved and had another baby.

I've turned it over and over in my mind. I guess I'm just so associated with that horrible time in their lives that my presence is a bad reminder. I mean it was my voice she heard in her ear for hours and hours. And I was the one with him in the hospital for four hours, just the three of us - Dad, me, and the baby. I think if I would've known this would happen, I would have gotten another doula. I mean, I wanted to support them, but not at the cost of our decade of friendship. They see other people who were at the birth, but not me. They even used the same midwife for their next baby! For me, it was a double loss - the baby and the deep friendship we had."

Over the years, I have experienced the loss and bewilderment that comes from doulaing friends. It makes perfect sense that you would want to share your skills with the people you are closest to. We want to help them have better births and supported births. I really learned the issues with attending the births of friends by encountering them myself, but it wasn't very clear to me until much later why these things happened. As a researcher, I have formally interviewed more than 60 doulas (and many parents) about their labor support experiences. Informally, I have heard and collected thousands of births stories. Only now, after two decades of listening, do I have some coherent wisdom to pass along to you about attending the births of friends and family members.

As doulas, we are able to shift and change how we respond to our clients based on their needs. We are still genuine, but at prenatal visits, we adjust how much information we give, how much emotional support we offer, and what our role is with her partner and other support people. As doulas we may hold back at times from saying anything. Our friends already know our opinions. They know our birth preferences and what we think is best. We can't change who we are; they already know who we are! If our friend has the same vision as we do, it usually works out fine, but if she doesn't, there can be conflicts.

First, she may have a different vision for her birth, but may not tell you what it is. She thinks you're an expert or know what is best. Maybe she wants to be like you. No matter what, her confidence is such that she doesn't say out loud what she wants. Second, she may tell you what she wants, but secretly feels you are judging her. This is much harder to deal with. This feeling of judgment exists inside of her and can remain unaffected by anything you might say. You can reassure her all you want, but the fact remains that she anticipates you will judge her choices. This can affect her labor and your relationship.

It can also be hard to divorce ourselves from the concerns about her family. Prior to pregnancy, we know her frustrations with her partner, her relationship with her mother, and even the things we don't like about her. Because we know her, we judge her and her family members. Let's be honest here, it is a human thing to do - to evaluate others and develop expectations of their behaviors. We just do. However, with our clients, it is a detached kind of judgment and expectation. We don't know that much about them, so it's easier to not have emotional responses to their behavior. When Monique described Dad being on the phone instead of supporting the mom, she judged it as too much time and got upset with him. Monique struggled not to let her emotions show and knew that if she spoke to him, she could not keep her feelings out of her voice.

I have no evidence of this in Monique's situation, but it's possible that a shy father might not want to interrupt the laboring mom and her good friend. With a doula that he hired, he will likely feel a lot more comfortable telling her what he wants. But with his wife's friend, things can get a lot more complicated - especially if they were friends before he came on the scene. There are really only three conditions where knowing each other ahead of time can be positive. One, if everyone involved has the same vision for birth; two, if everyone feels free to express differences with one another, and three, when the events of the birth go smoothly and close to the ideal.

In our doula role, we are not emotionally involved with our clients and are detached from the outcome. That is why they hire us - because of our knowledge and our lack of personal history together. However, with our friends and family members, we care deeply. We want the best for them - the best care and the best outcomes. We have an emotional response to every step they make along the way. I think we've all experienced the aggravation of, "If she wants to avoid a cesarean, why is she seeing that doctor?" Our training tells us to keep that emotion to ourselves. We struggle with whether to say something. Either way, we're screwed. It's just a matter of how! Either we're seen as criticizing her choices when we speak, or we keep it to ourselves. Then we second-guess whether we should have said something, usually until the baby's first birthday.

Probably the scariest part of doulaing friends is the fear of a poor outcome. Intellectually, we know that stillbirths happen, babies go to NICUs, and some mothers don't do well, but we don't want it to happen to those we love and care about. We also will second-guess ourselves for a long time afterward. Is there something we should have done or said that might have made a difference? This is part of the grieving process. Whenever you attend the birth of a friend or family member as their doula, you need to be willing to let that relationship change. As we have read in the doula's stories, there is no guarantee that it will be in a good way. We are also affected by what happens; we know that our clients' births affect us. We need to process what happens, take it in, learn from it, and let it go. Over time we develop our own coping mechanisms for typical labor scenarios that we experience over and over again, but that is no help when it's your sister, daughter, or best friend. This territory is muddy and scary, and we aren't professionals anymore. We are loved ones.

So do I want to tell you not to go to the births of your friends and sisters? No, I want to tell you to go into it with your eyes open. You need to be willing to let your relationship change and maybe even end. Labor and birth are massively transforming life events! We want to help and we want to support. But maybe the way we can support best is by being a friend, a sister, or a mother who knows a lot about birth, but not being their doula. It's going to depend a lot on who you are and who they are and what happens. Just as with birth, there are no guarantees and there is no risk-free choice. As doulas we are in the business of messy human relationships. We freely enter into our client's lives at the most intense times. When it's with people we know, we bring our own lives and personalities into that mix, too. Whatever you decide to do, be at peace with your choice. Know you don't walk this path alone.

NOTE: As a researcher, I know there are exceptions, that's why we qualify our findings with "many" and "most." Most often when doulas tell me their experiences with doulaing friends and family have been good ones, there are a few possibilities. One, the mother's vision and the reality were very closely matched. There were no adverse labor events or outcomes. A second circumstance is they almost exclusively doula their friends: people they know prior to pregnancy. They are not professional doulas and have different boundaries. Rather, they are friends who know a lot about birth. They are used to being attached to people and express their own emotions at a birth freely and without reservation. Closely related to the "friend doula" is the "neighborhood doula*." Neighborhood doulas are known in their social group as The Birth Person. Everyone knows what she thinks about birth and what her vision is. Many women go to her for her knowledge and support during pregnancy. There is no uncertainty about her preferences for a healthy pregnancy and a good birth. She has a lot of affection for the mothers and families she serves. She is respected and has a place in their lives as a wise woman, church member, or literally part of the neighborhood. Because of these different social circumstances, her experiences are likely different than the ones described.

*I use this term to distinguish this role from *community-based doulas,* who are usually part of a social service program that serves a particular community of women or geographical area.

· · · · · ·

Amy L. Gilliland, Ph.D., BDT (DONA), is an AASECT Certified Sexuality Educator, a psychology faculty member at Madison College, and a DONA International birth doula trainer. She has a certificate in Pre- and Perinatal Psychology and has conducted workshops on attachment and infant mental health for UW Extension. Dr. Gilliland has conducted research on men and labor support, and worked with hundreds of families during the perinatal period. Her research has been published in *JOGNN, Midwifery, Journal of Perinatal Education,* and the *Wisconsin Medical Journal.* She also publishes the influential blog, *doula-ing The Doula.*

Amy Gilliland

Photo by Peg Schumann.
Used with permission.

Chapter 13

Supporting LGBTQ Parents: Tips for Doulas

Rachel Hess, MS, CPD

In my role as a postpartum doula and a parent, I have been thinking how to best support LGBTQ (Lesbian, Gay, Bisexual, Queer[1], and/or Transgender) families. As a queer parent, I have experienced anxiety when choosing a provider or going to a childbirth class, thinking about how my family, my identity, and my experiences will or will not be recognized and respected. Luckily, I was able to choose providers, during both pregnancy and postpartum, who had previously worked with LGBTQ families. As a postpartum doula, working directly in LGBTQ families' homes and leading new parent groups, I have experienced making sure that I fully recognize everyone's unique family and that my groups are inclusive of all families. Many doulas and educators I know have felt at a loss as to how best to do this and have asked me specific questions around language and family structure. Even for me, as a queer parent, it has been a process of trial and error, which has at times been humbling. Below, I offer tips for working effectively with LGBTQ families. It can also be helpful to recognize that we all make mistakes and the important piece is owning them and moving forward.

These are tips about what it looks like to support LGBTQ parents and how it can be different than supporting heterosexual families. Certainly many aspects of new parenthood are the same: the sleep deprivation, the feeling that your whole world has been turned upside down, the unconditional love you feel for your newest family member, and the need for support. However, LGBTQ families often face additional challenges and have different strengths.

My main message to those who care for new LGBTQ families is this: be vigilant. Words have the power to oppress, but they also have the power to validate and strengthen. In addition to being thoughtful about

---

1. A note about the word "queer": Usage of the word "queer" has evolved over time. It's important to remember that historically, the word queer is a term that has been used to oppress LGBTQ people. This term has been reclaimed by some gay men, lesbians, bisexuals, and transgender people as a self-affirming umbrella term. Be mindful of using insider language as someone who is not part of the LGBTQ community. The most commonly accepted way of referring to lesbian, gay, bisexual, transgender, and queer individuals or families is "LGBTQ."

the words we use, we must also take care to listen and reflect back the words we hear a family use. And remember, many of the terms we commonly use in parenting contexts don't "fit" gender-queer people. For example, consider referring to "nursing" instead of "breastfeeding" because some clients might not connect with their breasts or bodies. If you don't typically use the term "partners" when referring to couples, start practicing now. You don't want to sound insincere or awkward when working with two gay dads. You want to put your clients at ease by normalizing their lives and experiences, not make them feel exotic or other.

Recognize People's Multiple and Complex Identities

As the long acronym LGBTQ suggests, people identify in all sorts of ways! For some folks, saying they are queer, gay, bisexual, or lesbian means they are attracted to same-gendered people. For others, queer means they are polyamorous. Being queer can also mean identifying as gender fluid. Thus, I try to be open to people sharing their identities and experiences, and I avoid making assumptions. Especially when doing birth and postpartum support, it is my job to ensure that people are able to bring their whole selves to our interactions, including their sexual and gender identities. I tell my clients that I am there to support them as new parents, which means I am committed to them being able to express who they are in our time together. So, if they have language they would prefer I use with them, such as parent names, pronouns, relationship terms (i.e., partner vs. spouse vs. co-parent), I encourage them to let me know.

Be Mindful of Parent Titles and Pronouns

In many situations, mirroring is a key way of making others feels safe and validated. This is especially true when working with LGBTQ parents. When I first meet with a family, I will ask each parent, "What pronouns do you use? Have you thought of what parent term you would like to use?" I never want to assume anyone's gender in any circumstance, but certainly not where it is my job to be supportive. This introductory practice also has a way of affirming the non-gestational parent's role (when applicable) to avoid the insensitive practice of designating one parent as the "real parent." Also, in a situation where families have adopted or used a surrogate, finding out how they have chosen to name the members of the extended family can be incredibly validating of their particular family structure.

Don't Assume Extended Family Support or That Extended Family Is Not Involved

This one works both ways. Many LGBTQ families lack their family of origin's support. There are a variety of reasons for this void, but for many LGBTQ families that reason is homophobia. This separation is often very present when babies are born and can be especially painful. There is also the practical matter that life is harder without extra hands. However, when I am working with a LGBTQ family, I also don't assume their family of origin does *not* support them because many families are fully behind - both emotionally and practically - their LGBTQ children. Some families also experience something in between, such as a family of origin that is excited about the baby, but doesn't fully recognize their partner as a parent.

Recognize and Celebrate Community and Chosen Family

Many LGBTQ families have a great support network. This is a strength built out of a history of oppression. I will always ask, validate, and encourage the support that many LGBTQ families will get from their communities. I try to help folks think of what kinds of support others can provide - be it food, emotional, logistics, etc. I recognize that for many LGBTQ parents, this community is a central part of who they are and how they plan on raising their children.

Respect and Be Open to People's Conception and Birth Stories

For many LGBTQ families, a lot of thought went into how to bring their child into the world, so it's important to make space for that story when (and if) folks are ready. I never ask a lesbian couple, "Who's the dad?" or a gay couple, "Who's the mom?" There are as many different conception stories as there are different kinds of families, so be open to hearing each one. The prohibition against assumptions applies here, too. I do not assume an anonymous donor at the doctor's office. I don't assume adoption. Instead, I ask questions like, "How did you guys decide to have a baby?" or even, "What is your conception story?" I have found that one of the best ways I can be an ally to LGBTQ families is to recognize and see all of who they are and how they became parents, and this requires recognizing their experiences of becoming parents might be different from the norm. For many LGBTQ families, conception and birth stories are actually very empowering. For some, their encounters with homophobia and ignorance throughout the process - from a medicalized conception to fighting for the legitimacy of their partner's right as a parent to be present in the delivery room - can be very painful.

. . . . . .

Rachel Hess is deeply committed to improving the lives of children and families in the greater Boston area. In addition to her work as a postpartum doula, she runs prenatal and new parent groups at Mama & Me. Rachel worked at ReadBoston, where she helped develop and implement a brand new program focusing on supporting literacy skills in babies and toddlers. She also worked as the Training Coordinator for Samaritans, a suicide prevention non-profit. Rachel is a CAPPA Certified Postpartum Doula. Rachel received her Master's Degree in Language and Literacy Studies from Wheelock College and her bachelor's degree in African American Studies, with a minor in Gender and Women's studies, from Oberlin College. She lives in Jamaica Plain with her wife, her two children, and a large cat.

Rachel Hess

Used with permission.

Chapter 14

Doulas and Surrogacy

Renā Koerner, CLD, CCCE

Darla Burns, CLD, CPD, CCCE, CLE

At Doulas for Surrogacy, we've had the pleasure of serving a wide range of diverse families who have benefitted from the amazing gift of surrogacy. Doulas working with surrogates encounter many situations, challenges, and triumphs that are specific to working with these unique families. Challenges faced by doulas at these births can include a planned induction or planned cesarean section, the doula feels caught in the middle between the different birth preferences of the Birthing Woman (BW) and Intended Parents (IPs), and transportation issues to the hospital or birth place. Additionally the IPs sometimes do not arrive in time for the birth, take a childbirth class, or stay at the hospital after birth to care for the newborn. Postpartum challenges for doulas can include working in a hotel room with IPs, a lack of baby supplies, and transportation issues with IPs. There may be breastfeeding challenges for the Intended Mother and formula may appear to be the only or primary feeding option. IPs often needs lots of bonding education, support, and encouragement from their doula. Sometimes the BW needs to care for newborn because the IPs leave the hospital or have not yet arrived, requiring more support from the doula.

Labor Doulas

Doulas serving surrogates are certainly challenged to check their biases, and they must be very creative and capable of troubleshooting the unique situations they may encounter. Working with families of surrogacy is definitely different than working with non-surrogacy families. For example, some Birthing Women have young children of their own at home, and their husband/partner may need to care for those children when she goes into labor. She may need transportation to the hospital if in labor and may expect the doula to drive her, which is out of the doula's scope of practice. The doula must discuss this issue at their first meeting.

Birthing Women have given birth previously and are aware of what to expect during the birth process itself. However, the Intended Parents often have little knowledge about the birth process and have probably not attended a childbirth education class. Childbirth education courses, in general, are designed for couples giving birth and are not geared toward the intricacies of the Surrogate/IP relationship, which may make it uncomfortable for IPs to attend. This may put added pressure on the doula to educate the IPs on the physical and emotional aspects of labor and birth. Some Birthing Women may have the desire to have a non-medicated and more "natural" birth experience; however, in many surrogate births, we have found the labors are induced and/or may involve a planned cesarean section due to various factors including the need for the IPs to be present and the high rate of multiples being born to these families. Doulas are often supporting the BW to help her achieve a birth that may not be ideal for her, while supporting the IP's decisions as well. This may put the doula in a position of feeling like she's "in the middle" because she has likely been paid by the IPs; however, her focus of support must be with the BW.

Postpartum Doulas

The postpartum period for surrogate families is rarely emphasized, discussed, or honored. It seems as if the focus of all parties is on the actual birth itself, and not on what to expect once the baby has arrived and the BW is recovering both physically and emotionally from the birth. Again, we see very specific and unique needs and challenges. Many Intended Parents are reluctant to take classes in which they would be surrounded by pregnant couples, including baby basics or breastfeeding classes. Lack of education creates challenges for the new parents and for the doula. Many IPs have planned for years to have a child and have experienced multiple losses and disappointments, so they may have not have allowed themselves to prepare beyond the birth itself. Some IPs have no basic knowledge of how to care for a newborn and may feel their only option is to hire a nanny. This is why we feel it is so necessary for all IPs to understand the role and scope of a postpartum doula, so they know they have options in postpartum support. A postpartum doula, instead of assuming care of the baby, can guide them as they become more confident in their roles as parents.

Challenges in the postpartum period come in many different forms, and many stem from the fact that some IPs have no understanding of what is needed to care for a newborn. Some IPs choose to stay in a hotel until they finalize paperwork that allows them to go home with their newborn. Sometimes, these hotels are severely lacking in items they will need during their stay. A small hotel room with no kitchen, refrigerator, or space for a bassinet or swing is challenging for new parents and postpartum doulas. Some IPs have not yet purchased receiving blankets, diapers, formula, and bottles. A doula can offer suggestions and assistance in purchasing items that will make life with a new baby easier.

Many IPs assume doulas will be able to provide transportation to doctor appointments and will gather needed supplies. It is imperative that the postpartum doula always work within her scope of practice and inform new parents that she can't drive them and that they need to seek out transportation services, or perhaps stay in a hotel near the hospital, pediatrician, and local shopping areas, so they can walk to these places. Prenatally, postpartum doulas can offer suggestions on transportation services and options of housing to accommodate the needs of the new parents.

Feeding methods is another area in which some IPs are unaware of their options. Postpartum doulas can educate new parents about the options of giving their new baby(ies) breastmilk instead of formula. We have discovered that many IPs assume their only option is to feed their baby with formula. Interestingly, many families coming from other countries bring formula from their home country because they don't want their baby to get used to our "sweet" formula here in the U.S.A. When we make initial contact with IPs, we inform them of the breastmilk options:

- Having the birthing woman pump and provide breastmilk for the newborn for a certain period of time, if she's willing;

- Purchasing breastmilk from a milk bank;

- Seeking out a reliable donor;

- Having the new mother work with a lactation consultant to induce lactation.

We have found bonding with their new child is often a huge concern for new parents. They often wonder if their baby will bond with them and what the best ways are to achieve that. Postpartum doulas can educate these new parents on methods, such as skin-to-skin, babywearing, and infant massage, to help promote bonding. Additionally, by postpartum doulas staying true to their scope of practice and not taking over care of the newborn, but instead educating and supporting these new parents to care for their newborn, we see that more bonding is sure to take place.

Tandem bottle feeding twins

Photo by Megan Cardi.
Used with permission.

From time to time, the BW delivers much earlier than anticipated and the IPs are too far, possibly out of the country, to arrive in time. In this case, it may be necessary for the BW to care for the baby until the IPs arrive. The birthing woman often was not anticipating having to provide this care. Having the doula assist with the care of the newborn can help alleviate extra pressure and stress. Again, this is a scenario that should be discussed by all parties in the prenatal period, so a plan can be devised and proper support can be scheduled. Additionally, postpartum support for the surrogate can be a huge help in her postpartum physical and emotional adjustment, and should be considered even when she is not caring for the new baby.

There are so many more dynamics involved when dealing with families of surrogacy. We have learned a lot about how to troubleshoot these intricacies and have learned that we need to have discussions with both the Birthing Woman and the Intended Parents about all the possibilities long before the baby is due to arrive. Having multiple plans in place can alleviate the stress on the Birthing Woman and the IPs when things go off-course. With a doula's help, the birth and postpartum period can be a joyful and peaceful time for all.

Renádoula Koerner is a mother, wife, friend, daughter, doula, and business owner, not necessarily in that order on any given day. She is a certified labor doula, certified postpartum doula, certified childbirth educator, certified Happiest Baby instructor, and a Reiki Practitioner. She holds dual certifications with CAPPA and DONA, and is also an author and speaker. Her goal at Integrative Childbirth Services is "Bringing Knowledge and Compassion to YOUR Birth." She is the co-founder of Doulas for Surrogacy and works to help the birth mother and the Intended Parents get the support they deserve. She is the owner of the Lullaby Lounge, a local resource center for expectant and new families. She also volunteers as the President of Doulas Association of Southern California, and is the retired Chair for the banquet that brings together the entire birth community for a night of recognition. She sits on the board of the Doulas of South Bay, a doula co-op in Southern California.

Rená Koerner

Photo by Ashley Burns Photography.
Used with permission.

· · · · · ·

Darla Burns has always been fascinated with birth and babies. She began supporting women in labor in 1990, but only realized in 2003 that there was a name for the work she was doing. She immediately took a training to be a labor doula, and then continued on this path and became a postpartum doula, childbirth educator, Happiest Baby on the Block instructor, infant massage instructor, and a lactation educator. In 2003, she created her first company, In Due Time

**Darla Burns
and Madelyn Grace**

Photo by Elizabeth Thomas.
Used with permission.

Doula Services, which offers support throughout the perinatal period. In 2007, her dedication to this work led her to become postpartum doula faculty for CAPPA, where she trains women on how to best support postpartum families. From 2009 to 2013, Darla volunteered as CAPPA's Executive Director of Postpartum Doula Programs,where she managed the Postpartum Doula Program and Faculty in the USA and Canada. In 2012, she co-founded Doulas for Surrogacy with Rená Koerner, to better support families through the surrogacy process.

Darla has contributed to several books, has been quoted in publications and magazines, serves on the advisory council, and was interviewed for the upcoming documentary *After Birth Project*. When she is not doing her professional work, she spends time with her husband and two wonderful children in Southern California.

Chapter 15

Working with Teen Moms

Kay Miller LPN, CLD, CCCE, CLE, CCTE, CHT

Working with pregnant and parenting teens is a great pleasure and blessing; however, it does present doulas with some special challenges. As a product of a teen pregnancy, a former teen mom myself, and now the mom to two teenagers, I believe that I have a unique perspective into the needs of teen clients.

Even though there has been a recent decline in the number of teen pregnancies in the United States, teen pregnancy is not going to go away. One in ten children born in the United States is born to a teen mom. Three out of ten teens in the U.S. will get pregnant at least once before the age of 20. According to the Gutmacher Institute, almost 750,000 young women aged 15-19 become pregnant each year. This makes up 11% of all births in the U.S. each year. Of those pregnancies, about 57% result in live births (of which less than 3% are placed for adoption), about 27% end in abortion, and the remaining 16% end in miscarriage. Regardless of the outcome of the pregnancy, the teen will need ongoing resources and support.

The statistics show that the cards are stacked against the teen mom from the beginning. Parenting is the leading reason why teen girls drop out of school. Less than half of teen moms graduate from high school, and fewer than 2% earn a college degree by the age of 30. Another tremendous area of concern is the fact that teen moms are likely to have another baby soon. About 25% of teen moms have a second baby within two years of having their first. How can we help teen moms overcome these odds?

Teens go through various stages of development throughout the adolescent years. They generally go through these stages a few at a time, and sometimes they go through the stages more than once. One of the theories on adolescent development was by Jean Piaget, a philosopher and knowledge theorist. Piaget viewed adolescence as a time in which a teen moves forward from thinking in a concrete manner to a more formal manner - thinking more abstractly, forming hypotheses, and developing better reasoning skills. According to Piaget, teens feel they are "on stage" at all times. They feel the entire world is watching them. When pregnant, this feeling intensifies for the teen mom. They become self-conscious and very sensitive to criticism. They also deal with the "invincibility fable." Teens believe they are immune to the dangers of unprotected sex, drugs, alcohol, and more. They generally think they can have sex without consequences. They think that others might become pregnant, but that it will not happen to them. According to the National Campaign to Prevent Teen Pregnancy, almost 50% of teens have never considered how a pregnancy would affect their lives. Teens also tend to focus on themselves, to the exclusion of others. They believe they are special and unique, that others cannot possibly understand their thoughts and feelings. They may also believe they are destined for fame and fortune.

Professor Robert Havighurst, a physicist, educator, and aging expert, was able to identify 11 developmental tasks that are associated with adolescent transition into adulthood. The adolescent must:

- Adjust to a new physical sense of self;

- Adjust to new intellectual abilities;

- Adjust to increased cognitive demands at school;

- Develop expanded verbal skills;

- Develop a personal sense of identity;

- Establish adult vocational goals;

- Establish emotional and psychological independence from his or her parents;

- Develop stable and productive peer relationships;

- Learn to manage her or his sexuality;

- Adopt a personal value system;

- Develop increased impulse control and behavioral maturity.

A pregnant teen will be concerned with the same developmental issues as her non-pregnant peers. Pregnancy can, however, have a tremendous impact on each of these developmental tasks. A teen mom is dealing with an adult situation before she has fully completed her own development. She is still developmentally an adolescent. She may be expected by some to act like an adult, but by others still be treated like a child. This leads to confusion and frustration for the teen who is already struggling to adjust to a situation for which she is likely not prepared. Pregnancy can have a stabilizing effect for some teens. Unfortunately, for many, pregnancy and parenthood may conflict with normal adolescent development. If the teen mom is confused about pregnancy and parenthood, she has a greater chance of experiencing crisis and frustration. A doula who is knowledgeable about the potential areas of confusion can better understand the thought processes of a pregnant teen and can help her better adjust to her circumstances. The pregnant teen's level of maturity, mental and physical health, values, cultural background, and her support system definitely factor into her ability to adapt to the situation.

Teen moms have special challenges throughout the childbearing year. These can include, but are not limited to, the following:

- Challenges during pregnancy: Access to prenatal care, poor pregnancy weight gain, pregnancy-induced hypertension (PIH), anemia, sexually transmitted diseases/infections (STD/Is), true cephalopelvic disproportion (CPD);

- Challenges during labor and birth: Lack of education, low expectations, lack of support, higher risk of death/serious complications;

- Challenges postpartum: Obesity, hypertension, low-birth-weight baby, risk of child abuse/neglect to baby, risk of high school dropout/living in poverty, educational issues for baby.

How can we, as doulas, reach teen clients? The good news is teen moms WANT help. A recent article in the *Journal of Obstetric, Gynecologic, and Neonatal Nursing* stated that teen moms want:

- Nurses, coaches to guide them through the process of birth and breastfeeding;

- Information about breastfeeding;

- Individualized care showing respect;

- Acceptance for them as adolescent moms;

- Support for birth partners and encouragement to be involved.

Since teen moms say they want help, that means our job should be easy, right? Not necessarily! Teen clients are a special type of client. Sometimes they are resistant to help, even though they need it so much. Sometimes they have a wall up due to previous experiences. Sometimes they have a gruff exterior. However, all teen moms need support, regardless of whether they realize it. They need specific referrals; early prenatal care; extra support during labor, birth, and postpartum; and breastfeeding support. It can be difficult, if not impossible, to find support geared specifically toward teen clients in most areas. Teens are generally thrown into childbirth classes with adults, where they feel out of place, are sometimes ridiculed, and are left out of various activities. Sometimes they do not have a support person in class with them.

When I was pregnant with my son, I attended a childbirth preparation class with the father of the baby at the hospital where I would birth. The other couples were in their late 20s to early 30s. They were all married and had careers. Even though I was very mature for my age, I was a teen mom, and I looked younger than I was. I remember during the introductions on the first night, having some of the couples look at me with what I perceived as disgust on their faces, some of them even shaking their heads at me. Throughout the following weeks, they did not interact with us much at all. They seemed to avoid us. I was embarrassed and hurt, but continued going to the classes because I wanted to learn all I could about what was about to happen in my life. As a nurse and educator, I have watched teen clients come to my classes and deal with situations similar to the one I experienced. Many times, the teen moms do not complete the class series. When they do, they tend to sit off to the back or side of the class, and do not interact much with the other students. I do my best to spend some one-on-one time with them, let them know they are welcome, and show them that I am there for them. It is not our responsibility to make the couples "gel" with each other; however, we do need to make each couple feel welcome, and we do need to pay special attention to our teens, especially when they are in the mainstream classes. When at all possible, help the teen mom find a class for teens.

There are special family dynamics that may be a factor in the teen mom's life. She may or may not be with the father of the baby. She may have a new boyfriend. The father of the baby may be much older than she is. She may not know who the father of the baby is. The teen mom's mother may be supportive, out of the picture, or be very overbearing. It is important that you, as the doula, address the teen mom directly, not through any of the various people who may be involved. You may be the only person who is treating her as the mom that she already is. You may be the only one helping her build confidence in herself as a mom.

Sometimes the teen mom has supportive caregivers. Unfortunately, many times caregivers can be insensitive to the special needs of a teen mom. When I was pregnant, I was blessed to have an obstetrician who treated me as an adult. He spoke with me directly, on my level. He listened to my concerns and answered my questions. I did not feel like he looked down on me. The nurse that cared for me during my labor was phenomenal. She was one of the nurses who had taught my childbirth classes at the hospital. She took very good care of me, and did not seem to have any problem at all with me being a teen mom. Because of her, I had a great labor and birth experience, even though I had no idea what I was doing. Help the teen mom take responsibility for her care. Help her format a list of questions to discuss with her provider. Help her realize that she deserves the best care possible for her and her baby. Help her be educated, so she can make informed decisions.

Because our society puts such value in having a "perfect" body and thanks to the use of photo shop in creating unrealistic photos of people, teen girls generally struggle with a negative body image. As her body changes during pregnancy, she may become very self-conscious. Remember, teens feel like everyone is watching them. Some teen moms try to diet during pregnancy. We need to provide education to the moms, letting them know they should expect to gain weight during pregnancy, and why. Explain where the weight goes. Use visuals, such as photos, PowerPoint® slides, and a pregnancy belly. Discuss nutrition; refer her to a nutritionist if needed. Have her keep a food journal of what she is "feeding her baby," so it can help her realize that what she eats during pregnancy is important. This exercise will also help her "own" what she is eating and drinking. Later, a teen mom may struggle a great deal with the way her postpartum body looks. Show them what a woman's body looks like after birth, so they know what to expect. This website shows untouched photos of postpartum women: www.theshapeofamother.com. Talk with them about realistic postpartum body expectations. Remind them they won't go home from the hospital in their skinny jeans, and let them know that's ok.

Many teen moms will choose to breastfeed when they receive appropriate information. Many will choose to formula feed. Some will choose to pump and bottle feed. Regardless of how she chooses to feed her baby, the teen mom will need to be educated on how to do it. The information they receive from us as doulas and educators may be the only accurate information they are receiving. Remember that it is not our job to influence her decision or make the decision for her. If she is pushed into a decision to breastfeed when she is not really comfortable with it, and she tries and it doesn't work for her, she may feel like a failure. Remember that you do not know the reason(s) why she is making a specific choice. We provide information, then support the decision she makes, whatever it may be.

Giving a general resource list is not usually helpful for a teen. If you hand her a long resource list, the teen mom may be overwhelmed and not know where to start. She is more likely to throw it out than use it. She will need specific referrals to federal and state programs, organizations, groups, etc. that can help her with her various needs. Don't do the work for her. Point her in the right direction and let her be responsible for moving forward.

Doulas have a drive and passion to share our great wealth of knowledge. However, it is very important that we are careful with how much information we share, so that we do not overwhelm our teen moms. They need good information, but delivered in a manner they can understand. The information needs to be given in short, consistent bursts rather than all at once. Written materials need to be at no higher than a fourth grade reading level. Models, posters, videos, and other visual aids are very helpful. Activities and practice sessions are valuable tools to use with teen moms. Use terms that are correct, and clearly and simply explain what each term means. For instance, do not assume the teen knows what you are talking about when you refer to cervical dilation. She may not know what a cervix is, much less what it means for it to dilate, and she might be too embarrassed to ask. Explain things simply, yet thoroughly. It can be a difficult balance to keep, but it is necessary when working with teens.

Where can we find teen clients? Connect with the pregnancy resource centers, social services, WIC departments, health departments, school systems, etc., in your area. If you attend a church that has a youth group, arrange a meeting with the youth pastor to share your passion of working with teens and what you can offer if he/she knows of any pregnant teens. Almost everyone knows a teen who is pregnant, or at least knows of one. Network with doctor's offices and clinics. Other perinatal professionals in the area can be a great resource. Let them know you are seeking teen clients. The more people who know what you do, the more word will get out. Word of mouth is a great marketing tool.

How will you get paid? Teen moms likely will not be able to pay for perinatal classes or doula services. Until insurance companies consistently cover doula services 100%, doulas working with teens may need to be prepared to offer their services at a greatly reduced cost or *pro bono*. There may be a grant or a program that doulas can use to be paid for their time. If a doula is working with teens through a school or community program, she may be able to be paid through that program. I do not think the teen should receive everything for free, though. She is going to place more value on something she has to pay or work for. Find creative ways she can "work" for her fee. Maybe she can do some paperwork for you. Maybe she can help you set up for a class you are teaching. Maybe she can do some community service or help out in other ways. By teaching her how to "pay it forward," you are helping her learn responsibility.

I worked for more than two years at a pregnancy resource center in my area. I worked one-on-one with teen moms, from the time they found out they were pregnant until their babies were one year old. Some of the teen moms asked me to doula them. I worked as their volunteer doula. I did not require the teen mom to do anything in return and was taken advantage of a few times. I would work consistently with the mom throughout her pregnancy. I would be on-call for her for weeks, and then when she went in to labor, she did not call. I would have no idea that she had even given birth, and sometimes I never heard from that mom again. Conversely, there were many teen moms I supported who were very appreciative and valued the service I was providing them. I have had some of them contact me when they were having another baby and request that I be there with them again. It was a great learning experience for me, and I am grateful I had the opportunity to work with so many teen moms during that time.

As doulas, we tend to give so much of ourselves that we can easily become burned out. We need to take special measures to prevent burnout. When working with pregnant teens, it is especially crucial that doulas:

- Set and stick to specific boundaries;
- Have good self- care;
- Take time off;
- Have an outlet for venting and gaining advice;
- Learn when and how to say no;
- Recognize and address potential biases;
- Have a sense of humor!

If we aren't there to work with our teen moms, who will they turn to? Will they have adequate support and resources? Don't let it come to that! If we take care of ourselves, we can better care for the clients we serve. We do need to be sure to take extra care of ourselves when working with teens, as they can be especially draining on our personal resources and energy.

Teen moms are some of my favorite clients. They have made me laugh and made me cry. They have energized me and completely worn me out. They have blessed me tremendously and impressed me with their tenacity and strength. If you have a passion for working with teen moms, make sure you are well prepared to do so. Take a training, such as the one offered by CAPPA (Childbirth and Postpartum Professional Association). CAPPA's Teen Educator training workshop and certification process is ideal for anyone working with teens.

· · · · · ·

Kay Miller has been working with expecting and new families since 1998. She joined CAPPA in 2008 and holds certifications as a labor doula, childbirth educator, lactation educator, and teen educator through CAPPA. Kay serves as Executive Director of Operations on CAPPA's Board of Directors (since 2010) and is CAPPA faculty. She was the Region 6 Representative for CAPPA from 2009-2011. She is a nurse and a HUG Your Baby Instructor, and is currently working toward her IBCLC.

Kay Miller

Used with permission.

Kay is passionate about educating and supporting women during pregnancy, labor and birth, and postpartum. She encourages women to receive education, do research, and talk openly with their providers. Her desire is to present positive, evidence-based information to families, so they can make the best choices possible in their specific situation. Kay has two amazing children - a son born in 1996 and a daughter born in 1998. She homeschools her children, and she and her children are very active in their church and community.

Chapter 16

Branching Out: Doula Care for Immigrants and Incarcerated Moms

Vicki Elson, MA, CCE, CD

My life as a doula has gotten a lot more interesting in the past few years since I started volunteering. First, I was part of an on-call doula program at an urban hospital, supporting laboring mothers I'd never met before. Now I'm working with incarcerated moms, some of whom I have had the pleasure of getting to know quite well over long periods of time.

I'm getting to know a much wider range of families these days. It's better than traveling the world in terms of having intimate connections with people from all over. I feel more useful as a doula, sometimes because moms lack family support, and often because the whole family appreciates a little bit of shepherding through an unfamiliar system or a difficult time.

What's it like to be a doula for a family you've never met before? You introduce yourself and do your best to gently fit in. You assess what they need and whether they want you - and if they don't, you don't take it personally. You make friends fast when they find out how friendly and supportive you are. You support bonding. Then, when labor is over and the mother recovers her ability to speak in complete sentences, you get to know each other a little.

Sometimes she says things like, "I couldn't have done it without you," and sometimes she says things like, "Please go away." Sometimes she says things you don't understand because you speak different languages. But foot rubs, shoulder massages, and encouraging words cut across the language barrier, and the ancient, loving art of labor support knows no bounds.

A few years back a nurse-midwife at our local tertiary care hospital asked our doula network to provide volunteer doulas. The hospital serves a lot of low-income families, including recent immigrants from all over the world. This was a wonderful program for a couple of years. We used a Google calendar to sign up for on-call days. It was a great way to volunteer - we were only on-call when we wanted to be.

We lost a little something by not having a prenatal relationship, but we gained a lot because we could serve families who would never have had access to doula care. It was a great education for new and experienced doulas alike.

Some of the midwives got in the habit of telling clients they would be calling in a doula, instead of asking the clients whether they wanted a doula. It turned out that pretty much everybody wanted one once they found out what we do! But most of the midwives never got in the habit of calling us at all, and it was hard to keep the calendar full of volunteers. The project faded out after a while, but perhaps it will rise again someday.

That experience taught me about cultural humility, the quality of respecting everyone, assuming little, and staying sensitive and positive. I have to continually critique myself to make sure I am acting as a true partner and not perpetuating power imbalances. Cultural humility is even more valuable than cultural competency, in which you strive to understand the cultures you serve, while keeping in mind there may be as many differences between individuals in one culture as there are differences between cultures.

It has blown my mind to watch demographic differences melt away as trust grows and friendship sprouts. I think that's really fun.

Now that I've been a volunteer doula with the Prison Birth Project (PBP) for four years, I appreciate the cultural humility framework even more. PBP doulas are very clear that we are not so much "us" serving "them," as we are equals struggling together with our sisters and brothers in labor, in undoing oppression, and in life. It's a privilege and a joy.

What's it like to be a doula for incarcerated moms? You need to be pretty centered and solid in yourself, and you need peer support or maybe even clinical supervision, because you find yourself spreading love in a world of pain that goes beyond the physical effort of labor. It's a fairly safe assumption that any given incarcerated mom has a history of abuse, poverty, and/or oppression. Many suffer from addictions and/or mental illnesses. It's helpful to re-read Penny Simkin's *When Survivors Give Birth* from time to time.

You see things that seem intolerable, and yet you see moms being brave. Incarcerated mothers suffer separation from their children and families. They sleep on thin mattresses and nourish their fetuses with prison food. They give birth under the surveillance of an armed corrections officer. In many states they are handcuffed or shackled before, during, and/or after labor and birth. Hospital staff may or may not behave respectfully toward them. They may or may not have loved ones with them at the hospital. You can see how a doula might come in handy.

But by far the hardest part comes later. After a day or so in the hospital, they return to their prisons or jails minus their babies. While other mothers are worrying about coping with diapers or colic, incarcerated mothers are worrying about custody. Their newborns go to relatives or to state foster care, sometimes after a few weeks in the NICU being treated for neonatal abstinence syndrome.

As prison doulas, we provide a weekly childbirth class, which is an important social occasion, as well as an educational one. We have private prenatal appointments, we are on-call for labor and birth, and perhaps most importantly, we make a postpartum visit as soon as possible after the mother returns to jail. We stay as connected as we can during the first weeks and months postpartum.

Like supporting labor, that first postpartum visit back at the jail is mostly about being present as the mother processes a very intense and painful adjustment. She is struggling to adapt to separation from her newborn. She is anticipating only periodic mother-child visits, or perhaps none at all. Some moms are wondering if they will ever be reunited with their children.

This sounds unbearably sad, yet a prison doula is honored to witness resilience and love in the most challenging circumstances. Some of us love to feel needed. We have to watch out for rescue fantasies, since our job is just to listen, encourage, and acknowledge. There's plenty we can't fix, but there's plenty we can offer.

If circumstances permit, many mothers choose to breastfeed during the day or two they are with their babies in the hospital, and then they continue to pump and freeze breastmilk to be picked up by the baby's caregivers. Our record is eight months of pumping. PBP's founders set up this program in the first year, showing evidence for its benefits, working with staff, and getting hospital-grade pumps donated. Moms don't call it "pumping," they call it "breastfeeding." They love their babies this way several times each day around the clock.

Childbearing can be an opportunity for transformation - that was my own experience giving birth at home, surrounded by loved ones and excellent midwives and doctors. Of course, childbearing also has the potential for trauma. You can see that for incarcerated mothers, the trauma/transformation potential might be intensified. I started doing this work because I care about birth, but it has become much more: an education in social and reproductive justice.

I am more acutely aware that the U.S. incarcerates more of its own citizens than any other country in the world. The rate of incarceration is growing rapidly, as the "war on drugs," mandatory minimums, corporate-owned prisons, and "tough on crime" rhetoric expands. The rate of incarceration is very disproportionately high for people of color, and the fastest-growing prison population is women. Four percent or so of incarcerated women are pregnant. Eighty-five percent are moms, and most were the primary caregivers for their children before they were jailed.

That's why PBP also offers a mothers' group for mothers of children of any age. Mothers support one another, and they also explore the bigger picture of what political, economic, or social factors are affecting their lives. Some become more active citizens, participating in efforts to reform those factors. We are adamant this work is about valuing the mother, as well as the child, no matter what's in her history (which is none of our business, and we don't ask).

As doulas, we ensure that pregnant, laboring, and postpartum women receive positive messages about themselves. In the thick of the physical transition to motherhood, those messages go deep. Incarcerated mothers, many of whom are survivors of chronic abuse or oppression, soak up those encouraging messages and healing can happen.

As doulas, we are witnesses to women at their most spectacular. We are the ones who say, "You were so awesome in labor! If you ever forget how strong and brave and powerful you are, I'll always be here to remind you." When a woman is faced with the challenges of incarceration, separation, and a difficult life after her release, it might help her to remember herself giving birth with good support.

I know that after my babies were born, I felt like if I could do that, I could do anything. I am grateful every day for the good people who helped me give birth with confidence and love because it set the stage for my life as a parent and as an adult. It's a gift we all deserve.

I actually really like going into the jail. Being a prison doula is even more satisfying to me than being a "regular" doula. It requires more creativity, more flexibility, more patience, to be more open-hearted and less judgmental. The relationships can get pretty deep and pretty sweet.

It's also more frustrating. It requires more willingness to put up with institutional protocols, more struggles with mothers' medical, mental health, or addiction issues, more alertness to risks, and more awareness of just how poorly our society cares for its most vulnerable members.

I struggle every day between focusing on the mother in front of me and focusing on the broken system and how to fix it. Before I started working with incarcerated moms, I was blind to what's wrong- and now I have a front row seat. I hope that as more people become aware of skyrocketing incarceration and its effects on families, more people will join the efforts to support those affected by it, either individually or systemically, or both.

We need to trade incarceration for more appropriate treatment for addiction. We need to shift the emphasis from "tough on crime" to "smart on crime." We need to reform the bail system that keeps poor people behind bars, and the plea bargain system that entices innocent people to plead guilty. We need to shrink income disparities, improve education, and do a better job protecting children and adults from domestic violence.

I can only do one little corner of it, so I do the thing I most enjoy - hanging out with moms. I choose to do my best with a tiny slice of the population. To stay sane, I have to release my attachment to the things I have no control over, and just chip away at the things at which I might be effective. (Sound familiar? "... and the wisdom to know the difference...") I have to take care of my body and take time to goof around, accomplishing nothing. I like to meditate, so I can quiet down inside and practice changing the channel when my mind is stuck.

My personal theory is that as long as love is flowing out, there's not much room for sadness to flow in. We can acknowledge suffering and do all we can to alleviate it, but we have to be careful not to let ourselves get so overwhelmed that we can't get off the couch. This is a job for teams working together.

There are only a couple of social-justice-oriented prison doula groups in the U.S. We're hoping to see more, and we're encouraging those who are working toward starting their own. At the same time, we are working toward the day when the U.S. creates healthier, more effective, more family-friendly (and less costly) alternatives to mass incarceration.

· · · · · ·

Vicki Elson, MA, CCE, CD, is a mother of three children, a grandma of two. She's a volunteer childbirth educator and doula with The Prison Birth Project. She has been a childbirth educator and doula for 32 years, and she offers a streamlined, accessible childbirth educator training called *Childbirth Education Essentials*. Her award-winning film *Laboring Under An Illusion: Mass Media Childbirth vs. The Real Thing* is shown worldwide. She has interviewed hundreds of mothers from all over the world about what REALLY works for labor, and the results are available as an illustrated downloadable e-book. She's working on a new film on the same subject.

Vicki Elson

Used with permission.

Chapter 17

Sharing the Love: Creating and Maintaining a Volunteer Doula Program

Rivka Cymbalist, BA, CD (DONA)

Every woman should be able to find a place where she can birth the way she wants, or at least the way her body leads. Today, in North America, this is often a difficult process, full of hurdles and hidden traps. Should she birth in the hospital? Can she find a midwife? Is homebirth safe? How much does everything cost? Who should she believe when she is starting to look into her options?

Many women with financial stability can navigate through the system and find an option that suits them, more or less. Given the crisis in modern maternity care, these women often come out of the birth experience with more questions than when they went in. If a doula was part of a woman's maternity care team, the new mother is more likely to feel that she was at least partly responsible for what happened during her birth experience. If not, she may need months to accept and process how her birth unfolded.

Other women are not so lucky. Women who are marginalized by our society do not have the choices others do. If a woman is poor, a recent immigrant or a refugee, a teen or a young single mother, has physical or mental disabilities, lives on the street - the list of reasons for marginalization goes on and on. Whatever the reason for their marginalization, these women need the support of a doula even more than most. They are often alone and need the physical support, advocacy, and resources a doula can provide. They are often restricted in the choices they can make for healthcare providers, and may not know that choices even exist.

Enter the volunteer doula. She accompanies the new mother through pregnancy, labor, birth, and beyond, providing resources and support. Have you ever thought about organizing a volunteer group in your city or community? How do you do it? What are the challenges? What are the advantages? What do you need to start an organization, and what do you need to maintain it?

There are different types of organizations, run in different ways. If you are starting a volunteer organization, think carefully about how it will work. It is often a good idea to get not-for-profit or charity status, as you will then be able to officially give out tax receipts for donations. It will also give you more credibility if you are applying for funding or making a proposal to work with another organization. If you choose not to become a non-profit, then your organization can be a simple association or a collective of like-minded doulas. Whichever choice you make about structure, your group will be working in one of three ways. A volunteer doula group can be linked to a hospital, another social services agency, or it can be independent.

Hospital-based doula groups are wonderful - if they have the full backing of the hospital. The volunteer coordinating is done hand-in-hand with the hospital maternity ward, and the doulas are hospital volunteers and take shifts to be on-call. The disadvantage can be that the doula doesn't have the chance to do prenatal meetings and provide the mother with companionship during her pregnancy. She meets the woman for the first time in labor.

There are several volunteer doula groups in Canada that are linked to other social service agencies, for example, to community single-parent family groups, women's shelters, or young mothers' homes. These groups are very beneficial to the women they serve, but because they are linked to a "sister" organization, they can be limited in terms of their flexibility.

Best of all, I believe, is an independently run volunteer doula group. This type of group can serve whichever population its members want to work with; it has no regulations from administrators; and it can change and develop in its own way and at its own pace.

Oh! That leads us to another question - money!!! How do we organize and maintain a volunteer group with no cash? There are two paths a group can follow, and as always, the biggest challenge is burnout (more about that to come).

A volunteer doula group can be made up of a core group of experienced, professional doulas who make their living from doula work and want to do "good works" on the side. Each doula can perhaps take one free client every two months, and if the group is large enough, they can easily serve four or five women per month. This type of *pro bono* work is common in areas like legal work, but unfortunately, not common at all in the medical/ social services fields. The beauty of this model is traditionally underserved populations can have the services of trained, experienced doulas.

Another model that works very well integrates a training program and allows students who reach a certain level of training to accompany clients on a volunteer basis. There are several challenges in maintaining this model:

- You need to have a training program in place;

- Coordinating clients and volunteers can be time-consuming;

- Each student doula should be partnered with another doula, so your woman-hours are increased;

- Mothers are getting care from less experienced doulas.

This model is more practical and functions better on a long-term basis. Young, eager students are dedicated and excited about going to births, and they know they are not ready to be paid. They can offer their services freely without emotional baggage. There are always students coming into the system, so there is no lack of volunteers (although the supply does ebb and flow with the timing of the doula courses, and with the needs of the students). The training program thrives because theoretical study is enriched with practical experience that can then be discussed and critiqued within the safe environment of the doula class.

These two models can survive, more or less, without outside funding. The first model is maintained by the good will of a core group of professional doulas who can donate a fraction of their time to underserved populations. This model will fail if there are too few doulas in the group or if their supply of private clients diminishes.

The second model is maintained financially with the fees students pay for their training. This model can fail if the doula trainer becomes overloaded. Teaching a doula course, coordinating volunteers, mentoring student doulas, and maintaining a private practice can lead to burnout and failure if balance is not achieved.

The answer to all these ills is funding! There are three types of funding: government, private foundations, and private donors. Government funding may be available, depending on where you live and what kinds of connections with municipal or provincial bodies you have. In my experience, volunteering in the area of women's health is not a big concern in government circles - they are happy to see us working for no pay.

Private foundations are usually more likely to fund a doula group, and again, it depends on who you know and what kinds of connections your organization has. There are women-based foundations, commercial enterprises, and even drugstores, airlines, and banks that offer funding to those who are willing and able to write grant applications and keep on top of funding opportunities.

Which leads us to the next question: How is a volunteer doula organization structured? How many people should be involved? What tasks need to be done?

A volunteer doula organization can be made up of as few as three doulas ... but they will probably get very tired very quickly! The group can start as small as this, though, and it will grow organically as the supply and demand increases. The minimum structure you will need for your organization is a group of doulas and a volunteer coordinator. The coordinator can receive referrals from agencies, clients, or other professionals, and assign clients to doulas according to availability, experience, and compatibility.

If your group grows and becomes a registered charity, you may think of creating a more rigid structure that could include a board of directors or an official collective. If you choose this route, you can start to think about assigning tasks for some of the group members. The most useful of these would be (in an ideal world!):

- Volunteer Coordinator, who is responsible for accepting referrals, assigning doulas, and coordinating backup;

- Doula Trainer, who is responsible for teaching doula courses and mentoring the students through their volunteer doula experiences with the clients;

- Treasurer, who is responsible for the money: writing checks, creating year-end financial reports, and completing yearly tax returns;

- Grant Writer, who is responsible for searching out possible grant opportunities and writing applications;

- Media Mistress, who is responsible for maintaining a website, social media presence, and links with other media;

- Events Planner, who is responsible for fundraising events and special workshops;

- Resource Liaison, who is responsible for providing resources for clients - legal, health, food banks, clothing, shelter, and so on.

How can a volunteer organization maintain its enthusiasm, numbers, and effectiveness over the years? I suggest two main rules to maintaining a healthy volunteer organization. One, keep your focus! Your mandate should be serving the women: no matter what else you decide to do - fundraisers, activism, outreach, education - the bottom line is that you will be accompanying women through their birth experiences. Two, bring in new blood and fresh enthusiasm. Doulas get tired; they have babies; they move on (to midwifery school!); lives change. Structure your volunteer organization around a training program, so student doulas get practical experience attending births (always with a partner!). This enhances the training program and provides womanpower for the volunteer group.

Montreal Birth Companions (MBC) is a great example. This group grew out of a training program in 2003, and it is still functioning very successfully, with no funding to date, fuelled completely by the enthusiasm and dedication of its members. MBC provides care for up to 125 women per year. This number has been growing over recent years because of the dedication of the new doulas who are becoming involved.

Another very important issue for the would-be volunteer doulas is to consider who you will be serving. So, who do you want to work with? What kind of community do you live in? Who touches your heart? Which women have come forward and asked for your assistance? It's best if a group of doulas decides to work with one particular group, for example, refugees or women struggling with immigration issues, teen mothers, mothers struggling with substance abuse, women living on the street, or incarcerated women.

You do not need to advertise the volunteer doula service! You do not need to spread the word about your services because you will find many people calling you looking for a different service than what you are providing. Remember, you are going to be providing free services to a specific group of women. This is not the same as a private doula practice that charges a sliding scale.

Which brings us to the next important question: How can we, as volunteers, avoid the two biggest challenges? Burnout and resentment are dangerous, and they can destroy a volunteer group. There are a few ways that these deadly infections can be avoided:

- Prevention: Make sure your group meets regularly and often, and that members get a chance to speak out about issues that may be bothering them.

- Clarity: Make sure everyone knows what her tasks are. If a doula is in the group just because she wants to volunteer at births, then no one should expect her to help with fundraisers or make phone calls. The volunteer coordinator should have a clear mandate, as well, and try to set up your organizational structure according to the mandate before you get started. This way, coordinating will be easier. I learned this the hard way. My priority was always getting the volunteers hooked up with clients, but I never had time to make a decent contact sheet for all the doulas, so I was the hub for contact info - not necessary and time-consuming!

- Be clear about the mandate of the group. It is not a good idea to serve women who can afford a private doula, but need to pay in installments or have other financial obligations they would rather meet. If you are serving women who absolutely cannot afford a doula, then the risk of resentment and burnout is much lower because the group really feels like they are making a difference, and not being taken for a ride.

- Take time off! Every volunteer doesn't have to work all the time. Make sure you don't have one or two volunteers who are always doing the work - they will get tired and eventually leave. And, in terms of taking time off - try to have fun together, as well as just working! A potluck, a movie night, a doula party, these are ways the group can casually re-connect or get to know each other.

Many of our volunteers feel their volunteer doula work is more valuable and more fulfilling than their private practice. In fact, there are several MBC volunteer doulas who choose not to practice privately as doulas, but instead have other jobs and volunteer as doulas "on the side."

Volunteer doula work is definitely challenging, but for the right person, it is important and fulfilling. The women we serve have a great need for a birth companion. Many of them have lived through trials we can only imagine, and they come to birth with great resilience and strength. It is truly an honor to work with our clients, and this movement is one I would like to nourish and encourage. To that end, I am available for consultation and assistance in setting up and maintaining your volunteer program.

· · · · · ·

Rivka Cymbalist has been involved in different aspects of women's healthcare since she was a teenager. She has extensive experience in first aid, herbalism, maternity care, health education, and volunteer work. Since she began working as a doula in 1997, she has witnessed hundreds of babies coming into the world. Of these, fewer than 20 have been cesarean sections, several have been twin births, and 95% of them have taken place in the hospital. She is director of Montreal Birth Companions, a volunteer organization that provides free doula services to refugee and immigrant women. She has been training doulas since 2004, and regularly accepts apprentices in her practice.

Rivka Cymbalist

Used with permission.

Rivka is also interested in organic farming and lived for many years on a small mixed farm in rural Italy, where she was the co-founder of WWOOF Italia, a volunteer organization that promotes organic farming. She was born in Africa, and loves to travel and read. She is married, with five sons, and lives with her family in Montreal and Italy.

Her book, *The Birth Conspiracy, Natural Birth, Hospitals, and Doulas: A Guide*, was released by Curioso Books in November 2011.

Chapter 18

What I Have Learned About Growing a Successful Doula Business

Kimberly Bepler, IBCLC, CPD/T, ICPE

Starting Out

To start...know thyself. It is best to know who you are and what you enjoy before you start advertising or putting yourself out there. You need to know the parts of doula work you like and the parts you are not so fond of (or not yet adjusted to), and proceed accordingly. You can find out what your strengths are by taking a good self-inventory. You can ask those around you what they think you will excel at and what they don't see you enjoying. You can also take some cues from the first jobs you did for certification. What was the easy fit? What was more challenging? Incorporate the most popular things said about you into your marketing materials, or at least the most marketable things, i.e., being a good listener is a wonderful trait, but it is probably not a good marketing angle...few families think they will need someone to listen to them until they do! You might use 'non-judgmental support" or another phrase to better convey this skill.

You will need a couple of essentials to get started - a business card you can hand to clients (or anyone!) and a basic website and/or Facebook page, where people can see a photo of you and find out more about who you are. They need to trust you, both with their babies and with their money. Do not leave the photo out. If you don't give people a window into your world, they will pass on by and find someone who will. This is intimate work. It requires a certain amount of public vulnerability. However, keep your Facebook page *separate* from your business page. Although they need a window into your professional experience, clients don't need an open book about you and all your preferences! Remember to remain personable, but professional with client families and the public in your business.

If you create a Facebook page, start adding people to your business page as fast as you can who do related work or have similar interests; these are your *future referral partners*! Post things of interest to potential clients. Ask for feedback when you have enough people to make your thread look interesting to some - around 100. Ask questions on Facebook about babies, birth outcomes, breastfeeding experiences, and what motherhood is really like. Women want to share this stuff (and some dads and grandmas do, too!), so give them a platform and affirm their responses. Don't forget to interact with those in the threads. It makes people feel heard.

Formalizing Your Business

You do not necessarily need to make a detailed business plan. However, you *will* want to set a few goals. Decide where you want to go with this work, and then set out on a plan to make it happen. Keep in mind that it usually takes one to two years before postpartum doula work can act as your sole income unless you are willing to do overnight care (which can be more profitable, but costs you in exhaustion and increased stress on your body and family). Inconsistent work/income is one of the biggest challenges facing a new doula. When you are working, it will be wonderful. When things are slow, you will wonder if anyone ever did like you, and you'll get scared that you will never pay even the most basic of bills. This is a short-lived fear, but crops up now and then during the *famine* portion of the famous self-employment feast or famine roller coaster. Don't worry; feast is usually just around the corner!

Here are some suggestions with regards to launching your doula business:

- Decide how your business will be set up (i.e., sole proprietor, LLC, etc.). Download business forms off the Internet or buy a package of forms to save time. Take a class or read a book on basic business structure.

- Decide how you will accept payments and set up accounting software.

- In addition to your website and business cards, get active on social media (FB, Twitter, Pinterest, etc.). Talk to people you already know and trust. Start working with clients, learning from each one.

- Log your expenses, mileage, purchases, education, etc. Keep track of everything in a way that *makes sense to you* - not just to your advisors; no one can maintain this for you unless you pay them, so pick a way that you like!

- Getting a related job can be extremely beneficial if you are thinking about doing postpartum work as a full-time career. Personally, I have found the combination of educator and doula to be a great one. I teach baby care and breastfeeding classes at a local hospital. After a few years, I also developed a class for twins and was hired to facilitate their moms' groups. Win, win,

win, win. If you think something will complement your work, go for it. Client families understand when you have another job, and the consistent pay can make this work sustainable much more so than doula work alone for many women. When you work in a related field, the marketing also happens organically (often without you ever having to say the name of your company), and you make inroads into the community that benefit both your clients and your potential referrals. A little secure income and you won't be so nervous that people will never call again. (They will.)

- If you are a hobby doula, don't worry so much about the business part. Just tell your friends, make a few cards, and see where the opportunities arise. I don't encourage you to do this work for free unless you know the recipients, are doing grant or subsidized work, or work for a church, charity, or non-profit, where families are truly not able to afford a doula, but they need the services.

- However you want to doula is fine, just be clear about what your expectations are before you launch. If you do a lot of work for free, more people tend to think they can get a free doula, and those of us who depend on the income really have to struggle to justify our prices. However, we all love those big-hearted doulas who volunteer their time here and there…and wish we had one of our own!

Thinking of Expanding?

Many doulas find the idea of working for themselves daunting and prefer to work with a group of women. Some options I see frequently are independent doulas providing backup for each other, partnerships, collectives, doula groups, or doula agencies. If you decide to work with others, come up with a written arrangement and try to cover every detail you might encounter. When and how you get paid (and when you don't), how you transfer work for a *pro bono* client, etc. What's the cancellation policy for your backup? The more complicated things become, the more you need it in writing. Even what seems like a simple setup can get very messy when money is concerned.

A word of caution: don't make a partnership out of an even slightly tricky relationship. It just isn't fair to either of you. Both parties will likely end up being hurt and feeling that the injustice was all theirs. Yuck. Avoid this like the plague. Even the best relationships can be ruined by money squabbles. Don't risk your livelihood on a shaky relationship.

Having my own company of 3-14 women in the past ten years has been a huge benefit in terms of spreading out the work of a busy doula service, sharing the load with client families who need more than one doula, and using everyone's strengths to support families in the best way possible. It has also helped to provide for many doula families financially and brings value to the work women do in their daily lives that sometimes goes without recognition. There are downsides to group work, however, and I recommend doing plenty of research before beginning a group where jobs and expenses are shared.

Find yourself managing a group? Be the cheerleader, not only for your clients, but also for your team. Be their biggest supporter. Give them autonomy (they will take it anyway). Pay them well. Thank them regularly. Value their families *over* their work. (They are usually mothers and their own children matter, too!) Bless them coming and bless them going out…some might even return to you.

Beginning to Market?

When you meet someone else who has a small business, think of talking to them about *their* business before you mention much about yours. If you approach your role as one of discovering great resources for your potential clients, you will become a wealth of wonderful information for your families. In the end you win a bunch of referrals for yourself when you collaborate with related services. The people you connect with will give you far more business than you can get from an ad, a booth, or anything else impersonal. It pays to take the time early on to invest in finding resources and building relationships with other businesses, specifically those that serve your clientele.

When you have a chance to share what you have been doing, share the **passion** you have for your work! Passion spreads, and people not only appreciate it, they REMEMBER it. Don't overwhelm them with enthusiasm, but don't be afraid to talk about what you love about your job either. Few people get to do what they really love doing, and get paid doing it. We should be pretty jazzed about that.

Play to your strengths. Advertise your best qualities and skills. Don't try to be well rounded - it doesn't pay off. Do the things that you like doing the most, so you can help people in the best way. Don't be afraid to specialize. It is another way for people to remember you. It won't limit you as much as you think.

Advertise from the client's perspective. Don't think about what you want to do, think about how the client *will benefit* from what you want to do. Be careful to word things that way. Be authentic, but emphasize this is not about you. Your service is about serving them, helping them be wonderful, and yes, it makes you look good in the process!

Network like crazy. Meet people. Ask them questions. Be interested in their answers. Follow up. Show compassion for every client, even if they don't hire you or they need something completely different. Treat them like you would want to be treated as a client.

Call everyone back. Be kind to them. Offer them your help even if you can't serve them. Connect them to others. You want to be a resource. Know whom to call. Take time to find out. Get to know the people in your area you can confidently refer to for EVERYTHING. Labor doulas, other postpartum doulas, lactation consultants, pediatricians, nanny agencies, craniosacral therapists, chiropractors, naturopaths, acupuncturists, massage therapists, meal delivery, grocery delivery, house cleaners…get to know everyone who can help the people you are serving! These are the same people who will likely refer you to their valued clients.

Know when you are the answer, and when you aren't. Be honest with people and tell them when you are not the best solution to their problem. They might still hire you.

Prenatal face-to-face meetings are a wonderful opportunity to "interview" a prospective family, as well as for them to get to know you. There is so much written about how to interview well, and I encourage you to read and practice the things you learn. However, I believe the best thing a doula can do is *really listen* to what families are asking or expressing to you. Responding to client questions is far more successful than launching into a prepared speech. Remember you are looking for a connection with your clients, and not just trying to get them to hire you. Connection is what helps them trust you and listen to you, and what gives us the satisfaction of making a difference in someone's life.

When you talk to a client on the phone, you need to really hone your listening skills, as you won't have body language to guide you. Listen for the key concerns in their voices as they express their situation:

- "I am concerned about my older child."

- "I am worried about breastfeeding (or breastfeeding twins!)."

- "I don't want to repeat what happened last time."

- "I am having a cesarean and worried about my recovery."

- "I have relatives who won't be able to help me."

- "I'm at risk for postpartum depression."

Respond to these with empathy (it always works!), and then offer some ways that doula service can help fill their specific needs. Give them options, but don't tell them how to use the service. You want to sell yourself as flexible, adaptable, and willing to bend whichever way they need. Just try to avoid being wishy-washy. People prefer confidence, especially when they are unsure of something.

Smart Doula Business Practices

Keep track of people. Check in with them. Return phone calls as soon as you can do so professionally (usually not when you have a tired toddler or dinner is almost ready). Check in periodically before the baby arrives, and then after if you don't get a request for support. Offer other things you can do or suggest other resources to support them.

Be flexible with your client families, but don't let them abuse your grace. Give them a window of time they need to get your services secured, a reasonable cancellation policy in writing, and a non-refundable deposit that you keep if they decide against using your service. Provide a contract or work agreement, and outline everything in your policies, so it will be there in black and white. Allow them to ask questions before signing it, and keep adding to it until you have taken into account all possible situations…now you have a stellar work agreement!

Follow up with people before you write them off for not responding. People get busy, overwhelmed even, and don't mean to not follow up. So you might just send them a quick email to say, "If you are still interested, please_____…" or whatever you think would work. If they don't respond, let them go, but if you are gentle, you might find they loved you and just forgot that you were waiting for their response. I have discovered many jobs this way, just by checking in with people. I have also found out they lost my contact info. Or they were actually not interested, which is good to know, too. (No problem; moving on.)

Be nice to people…even when you don't feel like it. That goes for your clients first and foremost, and for your team members a close second.

Keep your integrity, even when the client is wrong. Pay your partner/backup/team, even when you make mistakes or it causes you to lose money. Let clients not pay now and then. Take it on the chin. It always comes back, usually multiplied.

Tithe or give to charity; it really makes a difference in how well your business does, and it does your heart good. We've used this principle many times when we have experienced a slump. Every single time we have seen an increase in our business after giving, as well as an increase in our hearts. It is a joy to give; I encourage you to think abundantly.

Time is valuable. Invest it in others and not just clients. Invest it in other mother-owned businesses. Invest it in relationships with related businesses that will eventually benefit you. One of the best moves I ever made was to form a small networking group nearly a decade ago with other women-owned businesses in related fields. This has resulted in lasting friendships and loyal business referrals, which have remained to this day. Give it a try.

Invest your off time the way you want to, so work doesn't feel like it is cutting into your family circle. (I will let you know when I figure out what that balance is....)

How To Be Such A Great Doula That You Don't Need To Advertise!

Over-deliver on what you promise. Don't tell people you can work miracles, but don't undervalue yourself either. Be awesome. It isn't hard. You are already awesome - it is a common trait in doulas!

Offer specific types of help. Don't say, "What can I do for you?" if you don't know what to suggest. Your client might be feeling spacey, wanting people to read her mind, not feel articulate right then, or feel overwhelmed and can't be specific about her needs. Plan ahead for things you know you can do. Give her a few choices (not too many; early on this is overwhelming!), but be prepared for her to take none of them and ask for something else. I often say, "What do you feel like right now? Are you hungry, tired, or just need some time to ask questions?" It is often one of these.

Read her body language. The slightest movement toward her baby means she wants to hold him or her; hand baby over quickly. Watch her hands, her feet, her shoulder position, and her facial expressions. There are hidden cues here that allow you to ask the right kinds of questions.

When you are serving a family, compliment them. Find something wonderful about their baby, their house, their relationship. Ask fun questions that allow them to tell you some of their stories:

- How did you meet/how long have you been together?

- Tell me about your baby's name?

- How are you feeling emotionally about this experience?

- What is the most important thing you want to accomplish today?

Above all, honor who they are as this baby's parents. You will always be on their side. You trust them with their baby, and you will back them, even if other relatives don't agree (or even if you don't agree!). No matter what, this baby is their chance to parent *their* way.

Become their biggest fan and they will become yours! Then business becomes just something you have to maintain, and not something you have to work hard for. As most of us are made for serving and not for the more detailed work of operating a business, this is music to our ears. Zig Ziglar said, "If you want to succeed, you need to help enough other people find their success"…and that really does work in the doula realm. Plus, it is so satisfying!

Doula work can be a dream come true! I want you to succeed, so you can have years of serving families and realize the difference you can make in the lives of newborn families.

. . . . . .

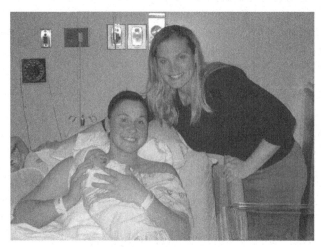

**Kimberly Bepler with
Sarah Stuurmans and
her baby**

Used with permission.

Kimberly Bepler is the owner and founder of ABC Doula Service. She is a Certified Postpartum Doula and Postpartum Doula Trainer with CAPPA, a Certified Postnatal Educator (ICEA), and a Board-Certified Lactation Consultant (IBCLC).

Kimberly founded ABC Doula in 2001, working with a passion for newborns and their families. In 2003, she incorporated into a group and loves the collaboration of the team that has come together (serving more than 1,100 families in the past ten years).

Kimberly teaches breastfeeding, newborn care, and twin/triplet classes, as well as facilitating new moms groups within two hospital systems, and offers beginning and advanced doula trainings through CAPPA. Her joy is in helping new parents *and* new doulas, so this is truly her dream profession!

Kimberly is the mother to two lively school-aged kids. She enjoys the support at home of her husband Mark, who manages the web and accounting aspects for ABC.

Chapter 19

Marketing Your Doula Business

Julie Brill, CCCE, CLD

Marketing is part of any doula business. Unlike yoga students or massage clients, our families use our services and then move on. Therefore, publicity, like laundry, is never done. Do something every day to promote your business.

Remember that every experienced doula was once an enthusiastic new doula, wondering where her clients would come from. She built her business and you can, too. Create an elevator speech that briefly describes what you do, so you can explain to people quickly the nature of your business. Practice saying it out loud until it flows easily. Be positive about yourself and what you have to offer. Identify any specific concerns you have about marketing or delivering your services. Develop a positive affirmation or two that helps you focus in on which direction you want to take. Write it down and place it in a prominent place, such as your computer screen, refrigerator door, or bathroom mirror, and read it out loud frequently. There is power in reading your affirmation, saying it out loud, and hearing yourself say it. For your business to succeed, you must believe you are offering useful services and be able to communicate what those services are.

Read *Selling the Invisible: A Field Guide to Modern Marketing* by Harry Beckwith. Doula services are, in Beckwith's words, something you are asking your potential clients to buy, "touch, taste, feel, smell, *and* sight unseen." Consider that, especially for first-time parents, their entire birth experience is an unknown, and they can't possibly understand how you as a doula can help them during their upcoming unknown experience. Beckworth describes services as having the distinctive characteristics of "invisibility and intangibility." It's quite possible that Beckwith doesn't even know what a doula is, but his advice for marketing a service seems to be written with doulas in mind:

> "In most professional services, you are not really selling expertise - because your expertise is assumed and because your prospect cannot intelligently evaluate your expertise anyway. Instead, you are selling a *relationship.*"

So as you converse with potential clients over the phone and by email, choose a place and an outfit for your initial interview, and endeavor to be prompt, professional, and warm. Consider what you are telling them about the potential relationship they will have with you if they hire you as their doula. One final point I want to stress from Beckwith's work is that your competitors are likely not other doulas; families are just as likely to be choosing between hiring you as their doula and choosing not to have a doula at all. So, in your marketing, as you sell yourself, remember to sell doulas as well.

As you get started, you'll need an Internet presence. Your website should clearly present what you offer and where you are located. Include an introduction to you, a description of the work you do, and testimonials. Post a photograph of yourself that looks professional. Ask friends and family to proofread your site and give you feedback. While many families hear about a doula through word of mouth, they often will go to her website to learn more. Start a Facebook page for your business; ask your Facebook friends to like it and frequently post relevant, positive information. Go online and look for services as if you are a pregnant woman in your area. List yourself on whatever free sites come up.

Connect with other new doulas in your community and from your training to support each other, refer to each other, and back each other up. Introduce yourself on local birth email and Facebook groups. If you have a niche you want to develop (VBAC, LGBTQ, Spanish speaking, homebirth, twins, teen moms, etc.), mention your credentials to work with that specific population. Do you have other related services to offer, such as belly casting, henna, placental encapsulation, caring for siblings at a birth, or photography?

Brainstorm where your potential customers are. Get permission to post fliers in maternity stores, toy stores, baby stores, libraries, coffee shops, chiropractor, OB, midwifery, massage, and acupuncture offices, birth centers, etc. Consider being a guest lecturer at a childbirth class, centering pregnancy appointment, chiropractor information night, or breastfeeding support group. Table at baby fairs; if this is cost prohibitive, share a table with others offering related services. Contact your local newspaper and suggest they run an article on your new doula business.

Participate in ongoing continuing education, so you stay current, meet other professionals in your area, maintain your certification(s), and have an increasing skills base to offer your families. With other doulas in your area, offer local meet-the-doulas nights or birth-professional-support teas.

Your satisfied past clients will be one of your best sources for referrals. Consider staying in touch with them by sending a birthday card annually to their children. Always ask new families how they heard about you. Follow up with thank you notes to those who refer to you and perhaps include a small gift card. If you are just building your doula business, but have a related skill (massage therapist, yoga instructor, childbirth educator, etc.), contact your clients to let them know that you're now offering doula services. Build a network of providers of related services, including lactation consultants, prenatal exercise instructors, prenatal massage therapists, chiropractors, midwives, and childbirth educators whose services you know you can recommend, and who will be likely to refer to you as well. Never badmouth other professionals.

We didn't go into this work to get rich quick, but in order to be fair to ourselves and our families, be professional, and not undercut others in our communities; it is important to charge appropriately for our work. Don't underprice yourself. Families are not necessarily going to go with the least expensive doula and may choose to pay more for a professional whose higher fees are indicative of her knowledge and experience. Consider your level of education and experience, the amount of money you've spent on your training, and your expenses, including childcare, website, and commuting, when setting your fees. Certifying doulas have expenses too, and don't need to attend births for free. Be ready to explain why you charge what you do.

Clearly state your pricing structure and refund policy. Some doulas state their fees on their websites; others email it during an initial conversation with a client. Having a strict written refund policy allows you to be able to say to a last-minute cancelation, "I'm sorry, but my policy doesn't allow me to refund you." Remember, you set aside this time for this family and may have turned away others to be able to serve them. Of course, you can always choose to make an exception if you are moved to by an extenuating circumstance.

Offer sliding scale, scholarships, and barter when it works for you. By clearly stating the value of your services, you are still giving yourself room to charge a family in need less, without devaluing what you offer. Volunteer for births when appropriate to give back to your community and gain experience. All money or barter should be collected before the service is provided. Families are only going to get busier and more hard pressed once their little ones arrive.

Build a structure within which you can give yourself raises. For example, a certifying doula may charge enough to cover her expenses, but increase her rate once her certification is complete, and again after she has attended another five to ten births or completed another perinatal certification. Invest back into your business. Keep your income in your business account until you have rendered services, and then set aside a portion to reinvest. Consider using PayPal to give your clients the option of using credit cards for payments and taking advantage of PayPal Credit if they need a payment plan. PayPal allows you to take payment directly from your website and to easily give refunds when necessary. Offer gift certificates. Perinatal services make great shower gifts.

Follow up with every potential client promptly. Families often hire the doula they speak with - or fall in love with - the first. Several days after an initial interview, phone or email to reconnect to see if you can answer additional questions. No one can be the doula for everyone. If a family tells you they've chosen to hire another doula, graciously wish them well.

Marketing and business skills require different strengths than doula work. Most doulas didn't choose this career because they wanted to excel at self-promotion. Yet, these talents are necessary to be able to get to where you want to be: a doula with a sustainable business, who is able to reach the families with whom she wants to work.

· · · · · ·

Julie Brill, CCCE, CLD, has been running and marketing WellPregnancy, her birth business, for more than 20 years. She strives to keep current with what works and what doesn't in today's market. She is passionate about people, especially women, being reimbursed for their time and expertise, and emphasizes marketing when she mentors new doulas and childbirth educators. Julie finds that the women who are drawn to doula work are an amazing group, and she feels blessed to be able to mentor, learn from, and work with them. Doulas' desires to support women during the childbearing year, pursue continuing education because of their drive to continually offer better services, and work unknown hours at unscheduled times serve as the inspiration for *Round the Circle*, her first book.

**Julie Brill and
Ella Martin**

Photo by Christie Martin.
Used with permission.

Julie is the mother of two teenage daughters. She has been homeschooling since 2001.

Chapter 20

Comparing a Retail Hardware Business to Building a Doula Business

Lois Brown Loar, Doula

When I was in first grade, my dad sold the farm to open a hardware store. Mom worked with him, running the office. Most of what I learned about running a business, I observed over the next 13 years of playing and working at the hardware store. The business grew from one small building to a building quadruple in size, with the addition of two large storage buildings behind the original location. Dad's income grew from four figures to six in 15 years.

Dad invested what he had to start small. He didn't invest all the money from the sale of the farm in the store. He saved enough for our family to live on while he and mom took no salary, but put the profits from the business back into the business until it started to show a consistent profit.

The hardware store carried high-quality products. If you bought something there, you could be confident it was going to last awhile, maybe even a lifetime. And if it didn't satisfy, the customer was given a full refund. Sometimes, that hurt the bottom line, but it paid off in reputation.

Customer Service, Customer Service, Customer Service

One thing Dad both said and lived was that he could sell the best merchandise available, but that it would mean little if there was no customer service backing it up. I saw him live that philosophy in many ways. I remember one night when winds were blowing and rain was coming down hard, Dad received a phone call from an elderly lady whose sump pump had failed and everything in her basement would soon be ruined. She had no way to "rescue" her property without a sump pump. Dad got up from bed, went to the store to get a sump pump, drove to her home, and installed the pump for her, keeping her basement dry and her property safe.

Dad offered free delivery to individuals in town. It was the attitude of going the extra mile that made an impression and improved his business reputation.

If Dad couldn't take care of a customer's needs himself, he saw to it that his employees understood and carried out his desires for great customer service. He did not take kindly to being even a minute late, even from his children. We understood that five minutes early was on time, and on time was late, because if we punched in "on time," we were not on the floor serving customers or relieving a fellow employee when their shift was over. All employees knew it was expected that we would do all in our power to help a customer find what he/she needed. Sometimes this meant making a special order for a customer.

Respecting Colleagues, Not Seeing Them as Competitors

Dad had an interesting relationship with the other hardware store owner in town. Dad had become friends with Mr. Riddle, and they respected each other. Fairly often, if Mr. Riddle didn't have an item a customer of his needed, he would call and we would take it to his store. This also happened in reverse. Even though each was the other's "competition," they recognized that both had a place in our community.

Give Back to the Community

Beyond customer service is giving back to the community. From the beginning, Dad gave all religious organizations a 10% discount on their purchases at the store. He donated merchandise and cash to both religious and nonreligious charities in town.

Dad was involved in local service clubs, not because of the exposure and networking it allowed him, but because he believed he had a responsibility to make his community a better place for all to live.

How to Apply Dad's Principles to Your Doula Business

First of all, start small. Invest in your business, but not to the point it risks your family's wellbeing. As much as I want my business to thrive and help provide for my family, it takes time to build a business to a level that one can draw from it in comfort, so I am investing my beginning earnings in building my business. Those earnings can be used toward marketing and further education for myself, making me of greater value to my clients.

High-Quality Products

Even though birth and postpartum doulas do not provide a physical product, we must take care to ensure we are providing the highest-quality service we can to our clients. This means keeping up with new technologies, such as apps for tracking contractions or baby's feedings while mom is napping, reading research studies on women's and children's health to provide evidence-based information to our clients, enhancing our skills by taking classes or going to conferences, and understanding we can continue to learn, regardless of our years of experience.

Customer Service

Customer service should be our "middle name." The word "doula" means "a woman servant." There is no shame in being a servant. A true servant's heart means putting others' needs ahead of one's self. I am not suggesting that we not charge a fair rate for our services. Simply that we should give of ourselves in such a way that our clients appreciate us beyond monetary compensation. I have had clients who gave me a gas card or some other gift on the last day of our contract.

Since our "product" is already service, how can we provide extra service? One way is to be entirely there for our client while we are "on the clock." Arrive a few minutes early, so you have your coat hung up, your hands washed, any new instructions, and you are totally ready to start work when your shift starts.

Look for extra things you can do that might make your client's life a little easier. If you are a birth doula, pay attention to the temperature and lighting of the room. Ask your client if it is good for her or if you can adjust anything for her. It's outside of "labor comfort," but it may be just the extra care that comforts her as much as positioning and encouragement. Look after the needs of dad, as well. He may be nervous and concerned about his wife's pain in labor. He may be hungry, but too worried to leave her side. Be there for both mom and dad, and step aside when those special moments between them are happening.

Before leaving a postpartum client's home, I let them know how the baby was while they napped, if she ate, was changed, etc. I ask if there are any errands I can run for them the next day. Yes, that service is on the clock, but to be proactive and ask if it is wanted is just good service. Sometimes, the errand is so minor that I don't charge for it. Just like my dad's free delivery, if I'm already driving past the grocery store or stopping there for myself, I pick up something my client may need.

Also, when encountering a needy client who may have difficulty paying for my service, there are times when a *pro bono* or deeply discounted

service is appropriate. A military discount is a nice thing to consider.
If you live in a military town or there is a local unit that is deployed for
several months, you may be afraid you won't make as much income. But
if you provide a great service at a discount to those who are providing us
a great service, you may end up with more clients than you can handle.

Respect Other Birth Professionals

Be respectful of other birth professionals both in and out of your
network or certifying agency. They work hard to be the best they can
be as well as you do. They may charge more or less than you do, or
they may have a very different philosophy of their service or how to
run their business. It's okay to be different. Different is not necessarily
wrong. What is important is that we treat everyone professionally and
with respect. Their experiences may be helpful when you come across
something you haven't done before. You may need a backup due to
unforeseen circumstances. Make yourself and your professionalism
worthy of the respect of others.

Give Back to the Community

Giving back to the community should also be a part of your life
philosophy. It is not just good business sense, but also character building.
There are many ways to give back. One is to speak at mom's groups or
teen groups. These girls have often not been nurtured themselves and
don't know how to nurture. They love their babies, but don't know how
to put that emotion into action. Being part of a birth or mom-and-child
centered service organization or offering seminars to a group might be
another way to give back.

Our Value

I believe our value is not in how much we charge for our services, but in
how we provide those services. Our character and service is our value.
Our fees should be fair, but flexibility is acceptable. Our best advertising
is our satisfied, contented clients.

· · · · · ·

Lois Brown Loar has been married to her best friend, Bob, for 39 years. They are the parents of 12 children, ranging in age from 15 to 38, and are currently grandparents to 17.

Lois graduated from the University of Toledo with an Associate's degree in health technology and worked as a medical assistant in an obstetric/gynecology office before her marriage and the subsequent births of her children.

Lois Brown Loar
Used with permission.

She is a homeschooling mom, with two teenaged children still left in the home. As she saw the days of full-time mothering waning, she sought to find the best use of her skills and experience. At the suggestion of her oldest daughter, a labor delivery doula, she researched becoming a postpartum doula. She is currently working toward certification.

Chapter 21

Do Yourself a Favor . . . Doula Yourself First

Charlotte Scott, NCLTMB, CLD

The phone rings at 3:00 a.m. Your client needs you to be able to help them feel calm and grounded. From sleep to game on can be abrupt. Your bag needs to be packed, your car filled with gas, and you must quickly put together some sort of nutritional support for a day…maybe two…maybe more? In the hours and/or days to come, you will be very present with your heart and your mind. You will put the laboring mother and her family's needs above your own. You will limit food and bathroom breaks to what is absolutely necessary. When a birth lasts for multiple days, you will be catnapping when the mother rests and staying alert and compassionate when she does not.

It's no wonder doulas tend to have physical issues related to stress, especially over time and with aging. Many of the full-time doulas I have spoken to show unexpected or unmanageable weight gain, high blood pressure, hormone imbalances, and other stress-related symptoms. Cortisol levels can spike extra high at night because we are sleeping "on alert" and not getting that good REM sleep. Our adrenals suffer from chaotic eating schedules and extended hours of little or no sleep.

The American Medical Association has noted, "stress is the basic cause of more than 60% of all human illness and disease." With constant stress, the body loses balance and starts to breakdown because it responds to all stress as if it is severe. It does not recognize the difference between small and large stresses, and constantly tries to adjust with a chemical response. It's very important that doulas embrace extreme self-care.

We do this because we LOVE our jobs and that helps balance the incredible demands on the mind and body. When you ask a doula why she does this work, her answer is usually "it's not a job, it's a calling." It is very fulfilling, heart-centered work. You want to keep doing what you love and feeling good while you do it for as long as you desire.

It is important to create intentional and therapeutic down time, the emphasis being on therapeutic. The day after a birth I immerse myself in self-care. I sleep as much as my body asks of me. I drink plenty of water, eat nutritious foods, and relax in my hot tub or my infrared sauna. I focus on doing activities I enjoy and make me feel good. It's the restore my body craves, so that I can repeat the process when the time comes. Our bodies need to replenish what we have taken from them.

I incorporate yoga and bodywork into my self- care regimen. Science is catching up and showing us yoga is very good for our health as it reduces cortisol levels and improves serotonin release, among other wonderful effects. I personally don't think I could do life, let alone my doula practice, without yoga. The beauty of massage, yoga, Tai Chi, or Qi Gong in between births is that it gives you a chance to focus on your overall health. It provides an opportunity for your "rest and restore" system to recharge.

I discovered through trial and error that I need to create pockets of time when I am not on-call. I make an extra effort to schedule times throughout the year to get out and immerse myself in nature. I love to kayak with my husband, and we find beautiful, serene, quiet spots and soak up all that nature has to offer. That goes a long way to restoring my body and mind.

When you can't get away, you can still use the incredible power of nature to restore your wellbeing. When the temperature allows, stand outdoors for at least 20 minutes a day barefoot. Walking meditation is an ancient Buddhist practice, but today it is known as "Earthing." The electromagnetic waves of the Earth help you feel grounded and energized. Popular health enthusiast, Dr. Joseph Mercola says, "Your immune system functions optimally when your body has an adequate supply of electrons, which are easily and naturally obtained by barefoot contact with the Earth." He describes it as the ultimate antioxidant. The other benefit derived from these 20 minutes of grounding is your daily dosage of Vitamin D. I have included below a link to the book *Earthing* by Martin Zucker, Clinton Ober, and Stephen T. Sinatra, in case you are interested in digging deeper into this fascinating subject.

There are some simple actions that cultivate self- care that go beyond the daily physical care a doula needs. We need to exercise, stay active, and eat healthfully for energy and stamina. We need to hydrate before, during, and after a birth to avoid long-term health problems. We need to learn to relax and restore in between births, AND we need to have an understanding of our own emotional care. If we ignore this area, all the other good things we do for our bodies will have diminishing return.

Three things I think go a long way to staying healthy:

1. Don't take it personally. This is not "MY" birth. Feelings of regret, remorse, or second guessing yourself only create a toxic environment within. Your body will store those feelings and they will become part of future births. There are situations that happen where you know you could do better, and other

situations that are beyond your control. Learn from the prior, and accept the later for what it is - beyond your control.

2. Birth is sacred. It is an event of phenomenal proportions. For the family especially, but also for the whole planet. A new person is joining the world. The reason this is so important is because it reminds us that there is a much greater plan, one that does not have to be handled on ALL levels by us. You don't have to control the outcome - you show up, are part of a team, and let LIFE work itself out. Trust the process, trust "all that is" by whatever name you give it, and trust women. We don't MAKE a good birth. We support birth in a good way.

3. Unpack your baggage on a regular basis. We all have it. Those things we store up that speak to us silently from the shadows. Birth has a way of triggering our issues such as:

    •   Feeling like women need to be saved or rescued;

    •   Feeling overwhelming anger and/or resentment at MEGA medical or patriarchal imbalance;

    •   Feeling self-doubt or fear of failure;

    •   Feeling you have to control the situation or have all the answers.

Many doulas are intrinsically sensitive - sensitive to the needs of women and the injustices women experience at the hands of medical professionals who have historically not trusted women or birth. It is what draws us to the work. Those sensitivities show up and get tangled up with our own issues, or they get triggered because of a recent birth - perhaps a birth gone awry or maybe witnessing an injustice. Processing makes all the difference here. Writing about it, talking about it with other birth professionals, and doing your own self-care will keep those bags unpacked.

Self-care at a birth is fundamentally important. The things you remind your client to do, do for yourself. First and foremost, hydrate! Take sips throughout the birth instead of guzzling every few hours. Have nutritious snacks to keep your energy level up. I like fresh fruit and green or energy bars. I also love coconut water; it keeps up electrolytes and counts for water intake. When I am really prepared, I have nutritious smoothies or soups made with super-foods that pack a lot of nutrition into a small package and can be consumed without much interference with the labor.

Please remember body mechanics. I cringe when I see someone trying to use their own muscle energy to support another person. I know it's hard when we've been on our feet for hour upon hour. Using your body wisely helps you last; the longer you are in a position of giving care, the more important this becomes. Pay attention to your posture and how you are using your body. Stooping, leaning, and generally supporting someone else's body weight takes a toll over time. I am a big fan of physics! I am a small person and 55 years old, so I find that I have to use my body in a smart way. Instead of demanding too much from my muscles, I try to activate my bones, and align and center myself in a way that gives me the most power for the least effort. Much like when you squat instead of bend over to pick up something heavy to save your back, you need to be aware of bending and stooping in ways that overemphasize muscles, and instead, bring your center of gravity back to your bones. Conscious attention to how we stand, sit, and walk gives you the most efficient use of your body's mechanics. Yoga is a great way to practice these concepts.

I like to keep my energy up during labor with my clients by dancing or doing a little Qi Gong energy boosting, coupled with a focus on alignment for both of us. Learning energy medicine, energy tools, and ways to keep myself grounded are one of my secrets to wellbeing in general. We have amazing amounts of energy resources within our own bodies; a virtual plethora of energy is available to us if we use our bodies and minds in a healthy way. We can access that energy by tapping into the body's meridian system and influencing our own energy or chi. This is the system used by Chinese Medicine and acupuncture. It is a river of subtle energy that keeps our internal resources boosted.

To learn more about energy medicine and ways to access your body's own resources, follow Donna Eden's work. She has been teaching easy ways to understand and use energy medicine for decades. I use many of her techniques myself and with my clients. For example, she has a technique called "Zip Up" that helps you clear up a foggy brain pretty quickly.

Get Rid of Old Energy and Make Room for New

Exercise helps boost energy levels. It can look different for different people. Gym workouts or private practice exercise and intentional movement help you move out old static energy and fill yourself with vibrancy. Yoga, Tai chi, and Qi Gong are mind/body exercises that can bring about instant de-stressing and help restore energy levels. You can learn a number of easy and free Qi Gong techniques on the Internet. I do recommend finding a class or taking a course, as that will help you really get the most benefits. I love to follow Lee Holden. He has shared a number of great shorts, like the "Qi Gong morning cup of coffee."

Don't Forget to Breathe

We tell this to our clients all the time, but it is just as important for the doula to be conscious of her breath. A deep, slow, intentional breath can reduce stress by activating the rest and restore side of our nervous system. You can use breath to pick up your energy as well. Long, slow, circular breaths energize your organs and improve blood flow to your brain. A few quick, energizing breaths, along with shaking your hands and bouncing in place, can give you a quick energy boost that avoids crashing and releases pent-up stress.

Do Things That Are Good For Everyone

Joining a laboring mom in dancing, stretching, offering energy boosts, and practicing breath awareness helps both of us feel calm, focused, and able to navigate the labor easier. Taking care of yourself during a labor is critical to endurance for the birth you are at, and also for those you will still attend. Listening to your body and responding to its needs are important and challenging when in a place of extreme support, so you want it to come naturally. Take care of your needs in between births and give yourself the support your body needs. You will serve your clients longer and be capable of enjoying your profession for a long time to come.

Be Part of a Community

I feel very fortunate to be part of a group of doulas. These ladies get me and have my back. I know if I end up with more than one mother percolating at once, I have backups who will step in. It is important to have support and a place to process both the joys and the sorrows of birth. No one else gets you like another birth professional. Sisters on the journey make the journey that much smoother, trust me.

References

Books:

Ober, C., Sinatra, S.T., & Zucker, M. (2010). *Earthing: The Most Important Health Discovery Ever*. Basic Health Publications. Describes the health benefits of Earthing, walking barefoot, and sleeping on the ground to experience the healing energy from the Earth.

Eden, D. & Feinstein, D. (2008). *Energy Medicine for Women: Aligning Your Body.* Tarcher Publishers. Describes working with subtle energies for health and wellness.

Eden, D., & Dahlin, D. (2012). *The Little Book of Energy Medicine: The Essential Guide to Balancing Your Body's Energies.* Tarcher Publishers. Describes energy medicine and how it works. An easy-to-use pocket guide.

Online Reports:

Heart Math. (2010). *How Stress Affects the Body.* Retrieved 2/12/14 from http://www. heartmath.com/infographics/how-stress-effects-the-body.html

CarePages. (2011). *The Basics of Yoga.* Retrieved 2/12/14 from http://cms.carepages.com/ CarePages/en/ArticlesTips/FeatureArticles/Contributors/basics-of-yoga.html

Links:

Mercola, J. (2014). *The Ultimate Antioxidant: Fight Premature Aging for Free.* Retrieved on 2/12/14 from http://articles.mercola.com/sites/articles/archive/2012/11/04/why-does-walking-barefoot-on-the-earth-make-you-feel-better.aspx

Holden, L. (2013). *QiGong -Morning Qi Ritual.* Retrieved on 2/12/14 from http://www.youtube.com/watch?v=zsbgidG4UNk

· · · · · ·

Charlotte Scott, NCLTMB, CLD, is a licensed massage therapist and body worker, a certified yoga instructor and certified labor doula, and a childbirth educator, teaching holistic practices to pregnant couples. She has been teaching holistic education and wellness practices, and working with women in prenatal and postpartum care for 18 years.

Charlotte Scott

Used with permission.

What Parents Say About Doulas

My doula is an amazing doula. I was still laughing with her during my labor. Five centimeters and big contractions! I think my daughter heard that and she is always laughing! I don't think people realize how powerful it is to have a doula present during birth.

Elizabeth Thomas, mother of Madelyn Grace

Having experienced birth both with and without a doula, I can attest to the difference a doula can make! We were lucky to have our doula at the birth of our second daughter. She knew exactly what was needed to help me trust myself to have the healthy, happy, peaceful birth experience my daughter and I needed.

Christie Martin, mother of Vivian Grace and Ella Faith

Before the babies came, I was unsure of the idea of a doula. I thought I'd want my own space and time with the babies. The true sign of a good Doula - and I was blessed with them - is that she comes into the home and the mother continues to feel at home and comfortable. We would not have made it through the first few months as gracefully were it not for our terrific doulas. I recommend to everyone - especially those having multiple babies - to enlist the services of a doula.

Stephanie Jane, mother of Sydney and Calliope

My doula was worth every penny and more! Calm, experienced and I cannot describe how important she was to our birth experience! A must-have at your bedside!

Jean Perrault, mother of Alexandra Rose

I will never forget how you heard the tears and fear in my voice that I was trying to hide. Having a postpartum doula (even just for one visit) helped my husband and me build the confidence we needed to parent our newborn. Your service was invaluable!

Maren Williams, mother of Ivor and Axel

Our doula's vast knowledge and kind spirit helped to make our son's birth less stressful for our family.

Martina Cochran, mother of Brody Glass

Our first postpartum doula visit was four weeks after our son was born, and it should have been four minutes. I learned more from our doula than from any book, birthing class, website, etc. I still tell EVERYONE that is expecting a baby to get a postpartum doula. I can't imagine how any of us would have survived without her knowledge and love for our family.

Jessica Fichtel, mother of Kai

We didn't know about postpartum doulas when our son was born 12 years ago (and paid dearly for it, with a heartbreakingly difficult 4th trimester). We hired a postpartum doula with our daughter's birth nearly seven years later - and it was an ABSOLUTE GAME-CHANGER. If we could have "married" our extraordinary doula, we would've done it in a heartbeat. Over half a decade later, postpartum doula care remains among the best (and smartest) money we have ever spent!

Camille, mother of Mattias and Helena

I was incredibly fortunate to have the help of three extraordinary postpartum doulas. As a mother of triplets, I never had enough hands, even with family around. My doulas helped me feed, change and hold my babies. They helped me get a shower or a nap. They cooked me delicious food. They helped me with breastfeeding and taught me all kinds of things that have made me a better mother!

Eve Bernfeld, mother of Hector, Rosalind and Raphael

Index

About the Author

Julie Brill, CCCE, CLD, owns and manages WellPregnancy in Bedford, Massachusetts. She began teaching childbirth classes and attending births in 1992, and mentoring new birth professionals throughout New England for CAPPA in 2003. She is certified to present Peggy Huddleston's "Prepare for Cesarean Birth, Heal Faster" workshops. She graduated from Tufts University, with a degree in Sociology and Gender Studies, and completed the Mass. Midwifery Alliance Apprenticeship Course.

Julie Brill and Ella Martin

Photo by Christie Martin.
Used with permission.

Julie believes passionately that birth can be extremely empowering for women, positive birth experiences set the stage for many other positive life experiences, babies benefit immeasurably from having the best beginning, and we all have the right to make informed choices about our healthcare. She is honored to have taught thousands of childbirth education students in a variety of settings, and hundreds of CAPPA birth professionals. She feels she has the best job in the world, and is blessed to have found her profession and her calling. Her writings on perinatal topics have appeared in *Midwifery Today, hip Mama, ePregnancy, Spirit of Change, The Boston Parents' Paper B.A.B.Y. edition, Parenting from the Heart, Special Delivery Magazine,* and *The CAPPA Connection.* She is a regular blogger at babyMed. She is the mother of two homeschooled teenage daughters.

Julie specializes in natural and VBAC birth classes. She strives to provide tools and accurate information, so each woman can choose the birth that's best for her. Julie believes birth is a normal, natural event which can be extremely empowering.

Julie finds the women who are drawn to doula work are an amazing group. She feels blessed to be able to mentor, learn from, and work with them. Doulas' desires to support women during the childbearing year, to pursue continuing education because of their drive to continually offer better services, and their choice to work unknown hours at unscheduled times serve as the inspiration for *Round the Circle.*

Dear Reader,

Thank you for purchasing and reading this book. I hope you enjoyed it and found it helpful. If so, you can help me reach other readers by writing a review of the book on Goodreads and/or Amazon.

Sincerely,

Julie Brill,

Ordering Information

Additional books can be purchased at
RoundtheCircle.com and on Amazon.

CPSIA information can be obtained
at www.ICGtesting.com
Printed in the USA
LVOW01s0456200716

497020LV00013BA/92/P